CONVERSATIONS WITH
MEXICAN AMERICAN WRITERS

CONVERSATIONS WITH MEXICAN AMERICAN WRITERS

Languages and Literatures in the Borderlands

Elisabeth Mermann-Jozwiak
Nancy Sullivan

UNIVERSITY PRESS OF MISSISSIPPI

JACKSON

www.upress.state.ms.us

The University Press of Mississippi is a member of the Association of American University Presses.

Copyright © 2009 by University Press of Mississippi
All rights reserved
Manufactured in the United States of America

First printing 2009

∞

Library of Congress Cataloging-in-Publication Data

Conversations with Mexican American writers :
languages and literatures in the borderlands /
Elisabeth Mermann-Jozwiak, Nancy Sullivan.
p. cm.
Includes bibliographical references and index.
Summary: Interviews with nine Mexican American authors
conducted primarily in 2007.
ISBN 978-1-60473-214-6 (cloth : alk. paper) —
ISBN 978-1-60473-215-3 (pbk. : alk. paper)   1. Mexican
American authors—Interviews.   2. Authors, American—20th century—
Interviews.   3. American literature—Mexican American authors—History
and criticism.   4. Mexican American authors—Political and social views.
5. American literature—Mexican-American Border Region—
History and criticism   6. Mexican Americans—
Intellectual life.   7. Mexican Americans in literature.
I. Mermann-Jozwiak, Elisabeth. II. Sullivan, Nancy.
PS153.M4C675 2009
810.9'86872—dc22   2008036159

British Library Cataloging-in-Publication Data available

CONTENTS

CONTENTS

STORIES THAT MUST BE TOLD
An Introduction

In a 1984 essay, Sandra Cisneros, now a longtime resident of San Antonio but then a relative newcomer to South Texas, records a Midwestern Chicana's impression of tejanos and their texts. A resilient group of survivors, she writes, their literature is "a testimony to the silenced (though not a silent) people: a literary-scape as vast and varied as the Texas terrain."[1] Cisneros's characterization of tejano writing equally resonates with Mexican American literature. Even today, twenty-four years after Cisneros wrote these words, this literary tradition, while thriving, does so without much public acclaim or significant recognition by the mainstream. Writing in a variety of genres, and experimenting with Anglo American and Latin American literary forms, Mexican American writers are marginalized culturally and geographically— they are, with very few exceptions, not part of the East Coast publishing industry as they live and tend to focus their works on the southernmost edges of the national borders or on segregated parts of the metropolises.

This hyphenated group of people came into existence with the 1848 Treaty of Guadalupe Hidalgo, which effectively ended the Mexican-American War. In return for fifteen million dollars, Mexico ceded a little over half a million square miles, consisting of the states of California, Nevada, Utah, and parts of Colorado, Arizona, and New Mexico. Texas had already been annexed in 1845. The treaty officially recognized the Rio Grande as the boundary between the two nations, and Mexicans in these territories faced a choice between accepting U.S. citizenship or moving south to Mexico. The majority of the people living in these areas did not leave their homes and instead faced the aftermath of war and annexation, which manifested itself in dispossession, random violence, and expulsion.

The product of conquest and domination, the borderlands, the areas north and south of the U.S.-Mexico border, became the spaces of intercultural encounter.[2] These "contact zones," in Mary Louise Pratt's articulation, defined as "social spaces where disparate cultures meet, clash, and grapple with each other, often in highly asymmetrical relations of domination and subordination—like colonialism, slavery, or their aftermaths as they are lived out across the globe today,"[3] speak to the disruption, dislocation, and displacement of huge populations, populations that suffered linguistic, cultural, social, and political disenfranchisement. Characterizing the border as an "open wound," Gloria Anzaldúa, however, goes on to say that the borderlands exist wherever "two or more cultures edge each other, where people from different races occupy the same territory, where under, lower, middle and upper classes touch."[4] This definition does not confine the borderlands to the areas immediately surrounding the geopolitical border, but it takes into account the migration of Mexican Americans from the annexed territories into the cities and rural areas all over the United States. This zone of conflict has, nonetheless, brought forth a vibrant literary tradition. Mexican American writers depict the borderlands as sites of cultural performances, multidimensional linguistic practices, and political consciousness.

As students of sociolinguistics and American literary studies living in a midsized city with a majority minority population of 57 percent Mexican American, and as instructors at a comprehensive, public, Hispanic-serving institution of higher education only 150 miles north of the Mexican border, we were interested in both the interrelationships among language, culture, and identity, and in contemporary literary responses to living in the borderlands, particularly within the context of current language, immigration, and globalization debates. To understand how literary practitioners view these issues, we invited renowned Mexican American poets, playwrights, essayists, short story writers, and novelists—Montserrat Fontes, Diana Montejano, Pat Mora, Sandra Cisneros, Benjamin Alire Sáenz, Helena María Viramontes, Dagoberto Gilb, Norma Elía Cantú, and Denise Chávez—to discuss their perspectives on the languages and literatures of the borderlands with us. We selected these writers because they represent different border experiences and hail from different border regions—the Mexican side of the Texas border (Fontes); the Rio Grande valley of South Texas (Montejano and Cantú); the El Paso area (Mora); Southern New Mexico (Chávez and Sáenz); Los Angeles (Gilb and Viramontes); and Chicago and San Antonio (Cisneros).

They represent a new generation of writers, scholars, and teachers, many of whom are activists as well.

In the process of demonstrating the presence of the silenced (though not silent) tejano writers, Cisneros points to a flourishing cultural production as she maps a literary tradition that includes Tomás Rivera, Rolando Hinojosa-Smith, Raul Salinas, and Ricardo Sánchez, writers intimately connected with the Mexican American civil rights movement. This generation, preceded by José Antonio Villarreal, often called the founder of Mexican American literature, including among the non-tejanos, and Rudolfo Anaya and Rodolfo "Corky" Gonzales, consisted predominantly of male authors. Not until the late 1980s did a significant number of female voices enter the arena, and our sample—seven women and two men—seeks to represent the contemporary Mexican American literary scene. Speaking to most authors in 2007 and 2008, we found that this group of literary artists has formulated an understanding of the borderlands that infuses contemporary American literature with a global awareness. Both in their work and in our conversations, these authors challenge narrow nationalist perspectives and stage various forms of transnational relations between and among Mexican Americans and Central and South Americans—economic, cultural, and linguistic.

These authors produce literature from the nation's margins, from the remotest parts of the country, and about people on the fringes of the social fabric. In their work, they seek to counter a pervasive sense of the "forgotten" border and its peripheral status in the national consciousness.[5] Unless the country is in the throes of anti-immigrant sentiment, as happens periodically and is currently the case, the border is an afterthought, Sáenz suggests. By re-siting and re-centering the border, the authors seek to produce an understanding of its centrality in the U.S. national imaginary—as Sáenz remarks, "almost *everything* that happens on the border matters,"[6] and elsewhere he elaborates, "I refuse to believe that my writing is parochial or insular and insignificant to a broader discussion of American letters or American culture or American identity simply because I write from this place called the border."[7] In this writing, we find stories of the invisible, the unheard, the exiled, and those bypassed by the riches of globalization: they are Mora's workers in the service industry who take domestic and seasonal jobs; Fontes's Yaqui Indians and the poor that live on "the other" side of the river in Nuevo Laredo; Sáenz's transvestites, Central American refugees, and migrant workers whose labor exploitation is obscured in a global market economy where a pound of onions costs eighty-nine cents in supermarkets across the country and around the world; Chávez's voiceless and abused female service workers in rural New Mexico towns who maintain their personal dignity by reflecting on the meanings of "service"; Cisneros's and Cantú's transnational migrants who continuously travel back and forth between Mexico and the United States; Viramontes's "despised and reviled"[8] californios—the urban dispossessed and indigent populations in Los Angeles; and Gilb's drifting, shiftless residents of the El Paso YMCA.

In their literary and activist work, the authors communicate their desire to counter the voicelessness of border subjects and the historical amnesia surrounding the border. Speaking of the Macondo writers' workshop that Cisneros founded, Cuban author Ruth Behar notes the group's goals of forging community and questing for a more just future by including "Americans of the other America, moving between cultures, languages, classes, homelands, translating our experiences for ourselves and others."[9] Cantú here argues for the importance of documenting the cultural traditions of Mexican Americans; she gives workshops to train and empower other Mexican Americans to continue this work. She also praises the activist scholarship many writers/teachers engage in and discusses the important work Mexican Americans do on the boards of, for example, an encyclopedia project. She found that the entry on "immigration" did not contain any references to Mexican migrations, a lapse she corrected.[10] Likewise, Chávez, in her interview, describes herself as being in the trenches of the community. One example of her activism is the Cultural Center of Mesilla, an arts resource center, workshop, and performance venue, which she founded to promote an awareness of border cultures and to foreground binational issues, such as the building of a border wall. As a Lila Wallace–Reader's Digest fellow, she gathered family stories and oral histories from senior citizens in Las Cruces for her project "The Divine Frontier/ La frontera divina." Mora's main concern revolves around literacy, and in her work on El día de los niños/el día de los libros, whose main goal is to link children with books, Mora notes the absence of children's books by Latinos/as, a lack she regularly brings up with librarians and teachers across the country. In our interview, she also takes on the literary establishment, as in the following: "In spite of all these comments about the 'Latin Boom,' or whatever, all you have to do is look at the numbers. For example, the Academy of American Poets does not have a single Latino on its letterhead—not a chancellor, not a member of their honorary board."[11]

These writers also, sometimes self-reflexively, take on this issue in their writing. In his essay collection *Gritos*, Gilb argues,

> Even after all these years, people like me are unseen, patronized, so out of the portrait of American literature. It seems impossible that so many of the writers I have known—and yes, me, too—with a decent record of publications by usual standards, still fight a battle for acceptance, that we are a product of an ongoing American story that is not foreign, not only about a dark exotic people, not only fascinating as so much is "south of the border," not just about the poor and dangerous other side of the tracks.

He also writes,

> Too little has changed since I went to college. A couple of new voices, a couple of new faces. No children from those working in restaurants and hospitals, paving the streets, building houses, cooking food, wearing hard hats, driving delivery trucks and wearing tool bags, washing windows, sewing, bagging trash and bagging groceries, typing and filing, answering office phones, picking fruit, picking vegetables, picking nuts, fitting parts, bolting, welding, sweeping, waxing.[12]

Actively working against neglect and forgetting, Soveida, the narrator of Chávez's *Face of an Angel*, becomes the repository of stories as she follows the advice of her grandmother's lifelong servant Oralia to "listen to the stories women tell you. They are the ones you should remember."[13] Similarly, in her latest novel, *Their Dogs Came with Them*, Viramontes's narrator highlights the importance of storytelling by the disenfranchised and the lack of scripts for such stories. About young Ermila and her girlfriends, she says, "The only things they cherished, their only private property, were the stories they continued to create and re-create in a world which only gave them one to tell."[14]

Justifiedly so, discussions of the borderlands have focused to a large extent on the domination by European Americans of Mexicans and Mexican Americans, and the reality of this situation must not be glossed over. What connects the writers featured in this collection, however, is their view of the borderlands as an international space, a space that cannot be summed up through the binary "Mexican vs. Anglo." A dynamic space of international exchanges and power relationships due to flows of goods and labor, the borderlands are the sites, the authors show, where colonization affects Latin Americans, Mexican Americans, European Americans, African Americans, as well as the various Indian populations. The U.S.-Mexico border is a transit zone where global migrations have left their imprint and led to new formations, culturally, linguistically, socially, and politically. It should be no surprise, then, that in the small New Mexico towns of Cabritoville and Agua Oscura in Chávez's *Loving Pedro Infante* and *Face of an Angel*, respectively, readers will find Korean shopowners, Filipino missionaries, Iranian scholars, soldiers from the nearby Fort Hood, and East Coast retirees right next to the descendants of Spanish-born hispanos. With close attention to geography, authors highlight the characters' placement in the world, focusing on the ways in which spaces are socially constituted, arranged, and managed in intercultural encounters. They pay close attention to the infrastructure, access, and spatial divisions of particular geographies. Such is the case in the one-half mile inhabited by Mexican Americans for generations in Viramontes's Los Angeles and subsequently seized by developers; the segregated space of the barrios called Chiva Town in Chávez's desert towns; and in the houses and manicured lawns where Mexican American maids come together with upwardly mobile professionals in Mora's work.

Space is prominent also in their use of multiple and binational settings, both in the United States and in Mexico. This practice serves to highlight Mexican Americans' transnational existences and frequently has the effect of casting a critical light on the United States. For example, the plot of Cisneros's *Caramelo* takes place in Mexico City, Chicago, and San Antonio. Like many Mexican Americans, the Reyes family in this novel takes extended annual trips to Mexico to visit family. From the perspective of the Mexican side of the family, Cisneros playfully and humorously, but nonetheless poignantly, offers a commentary regarding U.S. foreign policy as when Mexicans began to name their dogs Wilson after the invasion of Veracruz; the novel calls into question U.S. customs and mores as when the Mexican characters observe the "barbaric" ways of the U.S. Americans; or it critiques U.S. popular culture, when, for example, they express a fundamental dislike of Elvis for his refusal to kiss a Mexican woman.

While Sáenz unambiguously and unapologetically reminds us of the literality of the border (as geopolitical boundary) when he rejects its "troping" in current critical discourse, other writers embrace Anzaldúa's broader view that the borderlands are not restricted to the immediate geographical site of the U.S.-Mexico boundary but instead reach into the heart of the nation itself, its metropoles. Borderlands dynamics equally unfold in El Paso, as they do in Chicago, New York, or Los Angeles. They are present even in the heart of Iowa and Idaho, where considerable numbers of Mexican Americans have settled. Gilb and Cantú bring this to our attention, and recent presidential politics attest to this presence as well. "You carry the border with you," Viramontes succinctly states in our conversation.[15]

These authors internationalize the borderlands and infuse it with a hemispheric consciousness. This consciousness includes an awareness of the transnational entity of "Greater Mexico," a concept articulated by historians Colin M. MacLachlan and William H. Beezley, according to whom "the Mexican experience in the United States [is] an integral part of Mexican history."[16] MacLachlan and Beezley elaborate, "We believe that the history of the Mexican people in the modern era cannot be understood apart from events in the United States, just as the history of the American people must include the Mexican experience."[17] The concept of Greater Mexico takes into account the past and present social, political, and economic relations between the United States and Mexico, and also the cultural manifestations of the Mexican diaspora that resulted from the annexation in the wake of the 1848 treaty and the subsequent loss of territory after the Mexican-American War. According to MacLachlan and Beezley, the borderlands are a "vast transculturation zone."[18]

In their works, the writers demonstrate how intricately and in what manifold ways Mexican Americans are connected to Mexicans and other Central and South Americans. Cantú and Chávez dramatize this connection, for instance, through daily cross-border family visits and shopping trips. Sáenz does so by showing the ways in which the global is already present in the local. In his short story "Cebolleros," for example, the hotel that houses the onion pickers is a country unto itself with its own music, food, and traditions. As David Rieff calls Los Angeles the capital of the third world, Sáenz similarly demonstrates the borderlands as being constituted by different worlds that exist *within* the United States. Authors also highlight connections with other Central and South American countries by focusing on characters from a variety of nationalities, thus illustrating a 1993 query by the Latin American Subaltern Studies Group: "What are the boundaries of Latin America if, for instance, we consider New York the largest Puerto Rican metropolis and Los Angeles the second-largest Mexican metropolis?"[19] Such awareness of "this America" and "that America" finds expression, for instance, in the early stories of Viramontes and Sáenz, which both evoke the plight of El Salvadoran refugees ("Cariboo Café" and "Alligator Park," respectively). Soccer, a favorite game that unites Central and South Americans, functions in both Cisneros's *Caramelo* and Sáenz's short story collection *Flowers for the Broken* to indicate the various modes of interaction between people from the Americas. In the poem that concludes Sáenz's collection, the speaker, a Mexican American, reflects on the troubled lives of Central and South Americans, those seeking asylum and living in homes for the poor, and those haunted by fears and by unspeakable memories. Bringing together diverse peoples in the borderlands, Sáenz, Viramontes, and others construct a pan-Latino consciousness. In the words of poet Montejano, who rejects the term "Mexican American" because Mexicans, she says, *are* Americans, "somos de las Américas."[20]

The writers share a preoccupation with unearthing histories that are not commonly part of the U.S. historical canon. The rich history of Mexico, most saliently of the Mexican Revolution, becomes part of the texture of much Mexican American writing, as in Mora's poetry ("1910" in the collection *Chants*, for example) and Cisneros's fiction ("Eyes of Zapata" in *Woman Hollering Creek and Other Stories* and *Caramelo*). Despite its tremendous impact on the United States, manifested in huge waves of migration, there is a paucity of knowledge regarding the events related to the revolution, and Cisneros relates this amnesia to the colonization of Mexican Americans in the United States.[21] Fontes's historical narratives *Dreams of the Centaur* and her forthcoming *The General's Widow* focus on the Yaqui Indians' rebellion against Mexican dictator Porfirio Díaz's regime, as well as on Mexico's neo-colonial relations with the United States and European industrial interests during that time period. In her interview, Fontes said that when she conducted her research for these works, she found a distinct dearth of historical records in these areas of study.

As these authors draw attention to alternate histories, they also educate a U.S. readership by breaking up monolithic images of "Mexico" in the U.S. American imagination and by putting the regional and cultural diversity of the country on display. In *Dreams of the Centaur*, through her character Alejo's travels from the northern state of Sonora to the Yucatán, Fontes highlights the vast regional variations within the nation while in *First Confession* she delivers a narrative that provides the Mexican perspective on life on the border. Because of this regional variation and due to region-specific immigration patterns, Mexican Americans in Chicago may have very little in common with Mexican Americans in San Antonio, Texas, as Cisneros points out during our interview.[22] The writers contradict common first-world conceptions of Mexico as populated with indigenous dwellers, a view that James Clifford asserts is common of third world nations, and demonstrate instead the country's intricate connections with the rest of the world through trade—both economic and cultural—as well as migration.[23] In an earlier interview, Fontes asks, "Who has or has not lived in Sonora? We have Lebanese, Arabs, Sephardic Jews, Marranos, French, German, Irish, Japanese, Chinese and Mexicans."[24] Similarly Cisneros writes about Inocencio Reyes, the narrator's Mexican-born father in *Caramelo*,

> He did not know he was continuing a tradition that traveled across the water and sand from nomadic ancestors, Persian poets, Cretan acrobats, Bedouin philosophers, Andalusian matadors praying to la Virgen de la Macarena. Each had in turn influenced their descendant Inocencio Reyes. A low-ranking Baghdad vizir, an Egyptian cheesemonger, an Oulid Naid belly dancer wearing her dowry of coins around her hips, a gypsy holy man, a goose herder, an Arab saddle-maker, a scholar nun carried off by a Berber chieftain the day Córdoba was sacked, a Sephardic astronomer whose eyes were put out in the Inquisition, a pockmarked slave girl—the sultan's favorite—couched in a gold and ivory seraglio on the shores of Abi Diz.[25]

This global consciousness, echoed in Cisneros's assertion that she writes for "the Japanese reader,"[26] encourages a shift in thinking about Mexican Americans and the borderlands. She takes pains in the above quote to demonstrate the multiple roots of Mexican identity and illustrates Clifford's assertion that travel is part of the human condition. Likewise, Montejano speaks against a reductive view of Mexican American heritage and points to the fusion of Asian, indigenous, African, Moorish, and Spanish European elements. Or there is the relation of local events to the global—the daily war on the streets of El Paso that Sáenz relates to wars across the world in his poem "War (in the City in Which I Live)," or when the speaker of his

"Poems and Deserts and Borders" declares "I am an American," and goes on in a series of similarly structured identifications with peoples across the world to present himself as simultaneously Palestinian, Israeli, and Mexican. There is also the way in which Sáenz forges cross-continental connections between the Americas and Asia when in the poem "The Dead" he focuses on the migrations across the Bering Straits, questioning inherited versions of national identity and reconfiguring local identities.

Creating a new global awareness of border realities, focusing on the invisible and forgotten, and breaking out of the scripts available for storytelling are acts of transgression that find no easy recognition in mainstream culture. Likewise, the search for a language through which to express these experiences is not generally embraced by the public either. The authors in this volume show how linguistic hegemony supports political and economic domination, paradoxically countering the ideal of multilingualism in a global world. "In colonization," Viramontes states, "the first thing you want to destroy is the language of another people, the libraries of another people, the artists and the writers, and the intellects of another people."[27] Language has been used as an instrument of oppression in the colonized Southwest since the Treaty of Guadalupe Hidalgo. The suppression of Spanish has been poorly camouflaged by nationalistic and patriotic rhetoric promoting English as the language that will unite our nation and empower immigrants. Historically, concerns with high immigration rates have coincided with moves to make English the official language of the government. While not successful (yet) at the national level, there has been renewed interest in state legislatures to pass such laws. To date twenty-five states have passed official English laws. In states without official English laws, individual towns have found other ways to restrict language rights. Recently, Oak Point, a small town outside of Dallas, Texas, passed a resolution making English the town's official language, requiring all residents to speak English as a response to a recent increase in the Mexican American population.[28] In 2006, Farmer's Branch, also close to Dallas, passed an English Only ordinance that requires English to be the official language of the town and enforces a law that prohibits landlords from renting to non-U.S. residents.[29] This ordinance has been challenged by the Mexican American Legal Defense and Educational Fund (MALDEF) and the American Civil Liberties Union Foundation of Texas (ACLU). To get around costly court challenges, towns such as Taneytown, Maryland, have passed resolutions rather than making changes to town charters; Taneytown's particular resolution was titled "English Language Unity."

In the United States, underwriting the movement to make English the official language is U.S. English, a large political action group with ties to immigration reform. James Crawford,[30] a longtime critic of language legislation and anti-bilingual language policies, labels the push to make English the official language as "Hispanophobia," an outright case of bigotry. He rejects the argument that immigrants are resistant to learning English.[31] However, many parents buy into the belief that eliminating Spanish is the only way for their children to succeed. Sáenz sympathizes with families in this situation because "People respond to discrimination in different ways. They may be inappropriate, but they don't want to be discriminated against"[32] and, unfortunately, we internalize the way we are viewed by others. Sáenz captures these prejudices in his "Elegy for Burciaga": "They still think que somos medios rústicos—unless of course, we act exactly like them, speak like them, vote like them," which then allows Mexican Americans to be considered good citizens who have "overcome [their] gene pool."[33] Cantú firmly places the blame on the "mainstream culture [that] has negated the value of Spanish so deeply that even the mothers, the parents buy into it."[34]

Understanding reactions to linguistic suppression, the authors speak about the psychological effects of such domination. Viramontes is enraged because she has become speechless in Spanish, which she considers her mother tongue, as she was forbidden to speak it in the Los Angeles school system. She explains, "When you think about it, in the first five years of your life you are creating these images that are associated with the words—how important it is to know that your first introduction to the senses was in Spanish, and then to be ripped from that and taken away!"[35] Cantú and Montejano, among others, report having been "caught" speaking Spanish in school and subsequently physically punished. Fontes's braids were tied to a swing by a nun at her boarding school to force her to speak English. Additionally, Rodolfo Rodríguez refers to a report from the 1970s that showed that children in Texas had been forced to pay fines, made to write "I must not speak Spanish" multiple times, and made to stand on black squares.[36] Indeed, physical punishment for speaking Spanish is not past history; during our interview Cantú discusses a recent case of a Mexican American child in Idaho who was hit by his teacher for speaking Spanish.

While a global economy requires a multilingual workforce, language values as reflected in the U.S. education policies often index bilingualism, the expected norm in many other countries, as a handicap, especially when the other language is Spanish. Linguist Suresh Canagarajah comments, "We talk of globalization as ushering in a new life of border-free, unrestricted fluid relationships between communities; but knowledge itself is narrowly constructed, splintered along different communities, devoid of effective attempts at developing an intercultural understanding or a fair exchange of ideas."[37] Thus Montejano discusses the irony of being criticized for her lack of Spanish language skills as an adult: "When we grow older, all of a sudden there's a big demand for bilingual this, bilingual that, and you're wondering 'What happened here? Where did we go wrong?' "[38] We find that schools actively engage in linguistic terrorism by denigrating home languages and disallowing students to use them, even outside the classroom. In 2005, a Kansas City student was suspended for responding "no problema" when asked for a dollar (in Spanish) from a friend in a hallway. National president of La Raza, Janet Murgia, argues that instead of being punished this bilingual student "should be considered an asset to the community."[39] Sáenz straightforwardly remarks that the view that we should all speak one language is ludicrous. He says, "There are many languages in the world, and we shouldn't extinguish them. Some languages are endangered species, and we should protect them. Just because I don't speak indigenous languages doesn't mean that I shouldn't value them. That's an attitude toward language."[40]

In spite of the lack of support for Spanish language maintenance, a large percentage of the Mexican American population speaks it—29 percent of Texas households report speaking Spanish at home.[41] But it is not a simplistic choice of Spanish or English. The heterogeneous Mexican American population has appropriated many different codes. Gloria Anzaldúa lists a few: standard English, working class and slang English, standard Spanish, North Mexican Spanish, Chicano Spanish, Tex-Mex, and Pachuco, "the language of rebellion against Standard Spanish and Standard English."[42] Another linguistic code, often labeled Chicano English, is defined by Carmen Fought as "a non-standard variety of English, influenced by contact with Spanish, and spoken as a native dialect by both bilingual and monolingual speakers."[43]

Code switching, the alternating between languages such as Spanish and English, is the expected (often referred to as "unmarked") linguistic choice among many Hispanics. Mexican American authors capitalize on the richness of these language variations, frequently interspersing Spanish words or phrases. Mixing languages, a process Montejano prefers to call "braiding," creates innovative and boundary-breaking texts. The effect, as Lourdes Torres points out, is to "destabilize the established standard language" and to "break the rules of English."[44] These authors appropriate language forms in different ways for different purposes. Norma González considers "English as the medium of functional communication, of professional development, and of economic mobility. But with Spanish, the roots of feeling, of emotion, and of identity pull me back and tie me to a social memory. . . . Language is funny that way."[45] Montejano also associates Spanish with emotions—passion, love, romance, anger, and music—all communicated through Spanish. In Cisneros's *Caramelo*, the narrator, Lala, explains how her father goes to Chicago and tries to learn English. She comments, "The old proverb was true. Spanish was the language to speak to God and English the language to talk to dogs. But Father worked for the dogs, and if they barked he had to know how to bark back."[46]

Language, as illustrated in these authors' texts and their interviews, is closely tied to identity. Anzaldúa's often quoted statement best explicates this relationship: "So, if you want to really hurt me, talk badly about my language. Ethnic identity is twin skin to linguistic identity—I am my language. Until I can take pride in my language, I cannot take pride in myself. Until I can accept as legitimate Chicano Texas Spanish, Tex-Mex and all the other languages I speak, I cannot accept the legitimacy of myself."[47] However, she argues that a shared identity defines a Chicano/a writer, and not the content of the text itself. The "historical texture . . . a kind of borrowing from both the Spanish and English [creates] this Chicano way of talking and writing."[48]

Challenging the dominant view of the illegitimacy of their social dialect and the dismissal of their cultural history, these writers frequently go against the linguistic grain. González, examining the linguistic repertoires of Mexican American mothers and children, reminds us that "language can index both affirmation of self and resistance to minority status."[49] In a 1990 interview, Cisneros discusses feeling "othered" and silenced at The University of Iowa Writer's Workshop. She rejected such marginalization by purposely writing the opposite of what everyone else was writing about. She says, "Something very negative like Iowa turned out to be very positive because by taking that really antagonistic and very angry stance, I found what it is I could write about and no one could tell me otherwise."[50] In fact, it was then that she wrote the beginnings of *The House on Mango Street* and *My Wicked Wicked Ways*.

The complexities of cultural and linguistic "otherness" are frequently found in these authors' texts. Cantú, for example, writes, "En la frontera we are neither here nor there . . . And yet we are both here and there."[51] Mora characterizes this experience in "Legal Alien," where the Mexican American individual is tokenized, "sliding back and forth / between the fringes of both worlds,"[52] worlds where competency in Spanish does not give the speaker full access to Mexican culture and where mastering English does not mean acceptance. Finally, Sáenz writes "Someday, I tell myself, I will become a real Mexican. Someday, I will become a real American. In the meantime, I write as someone who is a permanent immigrant."[53]

Using Spanish in English texts is not without risks for both writers and publishers; in particular, the possible alienation of monolingual readers can mean limited distribution for a book. Cantú suggests that the difficulties of finding a publisher for her new novel is to a large extent due to her linguistic choices—her use of both Spanish and English. Writers who find their voices in bilingual texts and who will not make compromises for the monolingual reader must be willing to risk rejection by mainstream presses. All of the writers in this volume use Spanish and border dialects in their texts, but to different degrees and with different sympathies for the monolingual reader.[54] In *Gritos*, Gilb explains (in his oft employed self-mocking style), "Write from the gut and soul . . . Write from *las alturas* and from *hoyos* (avoid cheap, italicized, affected use of Spanish words)."[55] Considering the global reader, Cisneros often makes the Spanish text accessible through context, as evidenced in the following dialogue that provides the meaning of the word "conguero":

"And there was a certain *conguero* . . . "
"So Antonieta Araceli's father played the *congas?*"
"No. He wasn't the *conguero*."[56]

She also uses direct translation: "*Cuidate*. Take care of yourself."[57] While some of her text (and humor) will be lost to the monolingual reader, Cisneros's sensitivity to the different linguistic codes does attract a broader audience. In a 1992 interview, she discussed how it is Chicanas who will best understand and enjoy the subtleties of her texts. While she is sensitive to "people who don't know the culture," she says, "I try my best. I won't do it for the sake of an Anglo reader."[58] She uses Spanish without explication when it would be awkward to do so; then, she expects the reader to use a dictionary: "They can still get it."[59] In marked contrast to her practice in previous publications, Chávez included a glossary of Spanish terms with English translations in her most recent book, *A Taco Testimony*, after her editor and publisher recommended it. She says that her main concern in this book was that people get the recipes, whereas in fiction she would not feel obligated to include one. Sáenz finds the unwillingness to read texts with foreign words "ungenerous." He elaborates, "My response to people is, 'Why are you so ungenerous when it comes to other ways of speaking and looking at the world?' They have no answer because I reframe the issue in ways that make them look bad, because I am not willing to concede moral high ground to that attitude. Because it is very small and mean, and I've lived with that meanness my whole life in the United States. I refuse it and I refute it."[60] Both Viramontes and Sáenz expect the reader to at least work with and not reject the Spanish in the text: "Hell, if I want to be working ten years to give you this piece, please allow me to ask of you to open a dictionary," Viramontes says.[61] Finally, Gilb raises the question why the use of Spanish in English texts by writers such as Cormac McCarthy is widely accepted, but "It has never been considered equally exotic or decorative or literary for Chicano writers to do anything similar, but, ironically, only irritating."[62] McCarthy's Spanish is not italicized while the authors here find that they have to continually negotiate the use of italics with their editors for each book. Sáenz argues that one conventionally italicizes foreign words, but since Spanish is not a foreign language in Mexican American discourse, it should not be a marked variety. González affirms that "Language as symbolic of selfhood and of an 'imagined' community can be read as a marker of identity, the diacritica that both marks membership and resists the marking of the language."[63]

We are grateful that Montserrat Fontes, Diana Montejano, Pat Mora, Benjamin Alire Sáenz, Sandra Cisneros, Helena María Viramontes, Dagoberto Gilb, Norma Elía Cantú, and Denise Chávez so generously made time to speak with us. While our primary goal was to let them talk about their experiences as much as possible, our concerns with literature and linguistics, including issues around language policy, language attitudes, the relationship between language and identity, all guided our questions. In what follows, these authors discuss their linguistic choices within the context of language policies and language attitudes in the United States, as well as the East

Coast publishing industry's mandates. Defying all singular and essentialist definitions of Mexican American writing, their comments shed light on the multiple dimensions of borderlands literature—its at times stark naturalism, highlighting the ongoing colonization of the area and its people; its syncretic formations, blending Central and South American as well as European American heritages; its folklore, cultural practices, and spirituality; and its embeddedness in the mythology of the American West. Out of these interviews emerges a portrait of the borderlands as a dynamic space of international exchanges, one that is situated and can only be fully understood within a global context. We hope that the conversations will prove pertinent in light of recent national discussions regarding immigration reform and language policy and that they illustrate literature's ability to resist dominant ideologies—linguistic, cultural, social, and political—and to create shifts in perspective. We also hope that they will give readers a sense of the authors' personalities, their current preoccupations, their points of view, and their opinions on matters relating to life in the borderlands.

We would like to thank our student assistants, Andrea Montalvo, Mary Alice Salinas, and Chelsea Seiller, for their invaluable help with the transcriptions of the interviews and their bibliographic research. We are grateful for permission to republish the interviews with Pat Mora, Montserrat Fontes, and Diana Montejano. "Braiding Languages, Weaving Cultures: An Interview with Diana Montejano" was published in the *Journal of American Studies in Turkey*, Special Chicano/a Issue 23 (2006). "An Interview with Pat Mora" was first published in *MELUS* 28, no. 2 (Summer 2003). "An Interview with Montserrat Fontes" first appeared in *MELUS* 26, no. 3 (Fall 2001). Most of all, thanks to Joe Jozwiak for his critical insight, as well as his and Wes Adkison's unyielding support and encouragement.

NOTES

1. "Los Tejanos: A Testimony to the Silenced," *Texas Humanist* (Nov. 1984): 11.
2. For a critique of the term "encounter," see Norma Alarcón. The word, she explains, glosses over the "deadly collision that continues to kill and produce anger and grief in the context of multinational capitalist 'development.' " See "Cognitive Desires: An Allegory of/for Chicana Critics," in *Las Formas de Nuestras Voces: Chicana and Mexicana Writers in Mexico*, ed. Claire Joy Smith (Mexico City: Universidad Nacional Autonomia de México, 1995), 65.

3. *Imperial Eyes: Travel Writing and Transculturation* (London: Routledge, 1992), 4.

4. Preface to *Borderlands/La frontera: The New Mestiza* (San Francisco: Spinsters/Aunt Lute, 1987).

5. See also Debra Ann Castillo and Maria Socorro Tabuenca Córdoba's observation that the border is peripheral for *both* the United States and Mexico. *Border Women: Writing from La Frontera* (Minneapolis: University of Minnesota Press, 2002), 5.

6. "Notes from Another Country," http://www.benjaminaliresaenz.com/Pages/BenHome .html.

7. "Notes from the City in Which I Live: Poetry and the Political Imagination," *Elegies in Blue* (El Paso: Cinco Puntos Press, 2002), 95–114.108.

8. Sandra Cisneros, on the book jacket of *Their Dogs Came with Them*, by Helena María Viramontes (New York: Atria Books, 2007).

9. Vicente Lozano, "The Macondo Workshop: Latino Writers Come Home to San Antonio," *Poets and Writers* (March/April 2007): 70.

10. See interview in this book, page 134.

11. See interview in this book, page 43.

12. "Introduction," *Gritos: Essays* (New York: Grove Press, 2003), x; xii.

13. (New York: Warner Books, 1994), 137.

14. (New York: Atria Books, 2007), 61–62.

15. See interview in this book, page 85.

16. Colin M MacLachlan and William H. Beezley, *El Gran Pueblo: A History of Greater Mexico* (3rd ed., Upper Saddle River, NJ: Prentice Hall, 2004), xx. See also José E. Limón who, in his *American Encounters: Greater Mexico, the United States, and the Erotics of Culture* (Boston: Beacon Press, 1998) examines the entwined and ambivalent relationship between the two sides of the border. The term was coined by Américo Paredes to refer to "all the areas inhabited by people of a Mexican culture—not only within the present limits of the Republic of Mexico but in the United States as well—in a cultural rather than a political sense." *A Texas-Mexican Cancionero* (Urbana: University of Illinois Press, 1976), xiv.

17. Ibid.

18. Ibid., 432.

19. "Founding Statement," *Dispositio/n* 19, no. 46 (1994): 8.

20. See page 33 of present book. Pointing out such connections and revising nationalist thinking to include pan-hemispheric considerations, is not meant in any way to suggest a new and unitary pan-Latino/a identity. In *Caramelo* Sandra Cisneros humorously deals with the divisions among Mexican Americans and Mexicans, while taking a more serious approach to them in our conversation (see page 71), and Norma Alarcón takes an academic conference in Mexico as the occasion to highlight the gaps between Chicanas and Mexican scholars.

21. See interview in this book, page 68.

22. See interview in this book, page 73.

23. In his study *Routes: Travel and Translation in the Late Twentieth Century*, Clifford challenges traditional ethnography's assumptions of indigenous populations as "dwellers" and Western fieldworkers as travelers (Cambridge: Harvard University Press, 1997).

24. Roberto Cantú, "Without Points of Punctures: An Interview with Montserrat Fontes," *Journal of Literature and the Arts* 4, nos. 1–2 (1997): 9.

25. Cisneros, *Caramelo* (New York: Vintage Books, 2003), 199.

26. See interview in this book, page 71.

27. See interview in this book, page 85.

28. Shelly Slater, "Oak Point Proposes Language Barrier," WFAA-TV, June 2, 2007, http://www.wfaa.com/sharedcontent/dws/wfaa/latestnews/stories/wfaa070601_wz_englishonly.840d65b.html.

29. See official resolution at: http://clearinghouse.wustl.edu/chDocs/public/IM-TX-0001-0003.pdf.

30. For more information concerning language policies, see "James Crawford's Language Policy Website and Emporium," http://ourworld.compuserve.com/homepages/JWCrawford/.

31. A report released by the Pew Hispanic Center similarly questions this claim. Researchers found that 23 percent of first-generation immigrants say they speak English well, 88 percent of second, and 94 percent of third-generation immigrants. See Julia Preston, "Latino Immigrants' Children found Grasping English," *New York Times*, November 30, 2007, A12.

32. See interview in this book, page 50.

33. "Elegy for Burciaga," *Elegies in Blue*, 49.

34. See interview in this book, page 126.

35. See interview in this book, page 88.

36. Texas State Historical Association, *Handbook of Texas Online*, June 2, 2007, http://www.tsha.org/handbook/online/articles/BB/khb2.html.

37. *Reclaiming the Local in Language Policy and Practice* (New York: Lawrence Erlbaum, 2005), xiv.

38. See interview in this book, page 28.

39. T. R. Reid, "Spanish at School Translates to Suspension," *Washington Post*, December 9, 2005, A03.

40. See interview in this book, page 51.

41. Census Bureau Public Information Office, July 16, 2007, http://www.census.gov/Press-Release/www/2007/cb07ff-14.pdf.

42. *Borderlands*, 77.

43. *Chicano English in Context* (New York: Palgrave Macmillan, 2003), 1.

44. "In the Contact Zone: Code-switching Strategies by Latino/a Writer," *MELUS* 32, no. 1 (2007): 76.

45. *I Am My Language: Discourses of Women and Children in the Borderlands* (Tuscon: University of Arizona Press, 2001), 128.

46. Cisneros, *Caramelo*, 208.

47. *Borderlands*, 81.

48. Hector A. Torres, *Conversations with Contemporary Chicana and Chicano Writers* (Albuquerque: University of New Mexico Press, 2007), 127.

49. González, *I Am My Language*, 193.

50. Torres, *Conversations*, 200.

51. "Two Countries," *Poemas del desierto*, http://www.iesa.gob.mx/sonarida/24/poemas_desierto.htm.

52. *Chants* (Houston: Arte Público Press, 1985), 60.

53. "Notes from Another Country," 12.

54. See Lourdes Torres for a typology of linguistic mixing. She discusses strategies on a scale, from those that ensure easy access, including transparent or "cushioned" Spanish, to those that gratify the bilingual reader, and finally those that employ radical bilingualism.

55. Gilb, "Notes on Lit from the Americas," in *Gritos*, 146.

56. Cisneros, *Caramelo*, 270.

57. Ibid., 153.

58. Reed Way Dasenbrook and Feroza Jussawalla, *Interviews with Writers of the Postcolonial World* (Jackson: University Press of Mississippi, 1992), 290.

59. Ibid.

60. See interview in this book, page 51.

61. See interview in this book, page 89.

62. Gilb, *Gritos*, 119.

63. González, *I Am My Language*, 195.

CONVERSATIONS WITH
MEXICAN AMERICAN WRITERS

Montserrat Fontes, © Arnold Rubinoff

"THE STUFF THAT YOU PULL OUT OF YOUR *KISCHKAS*"

Conversation with Montserrat Fontes

Montserrat Fontes is a renowned novelist, screenwriter, journalist, and teacher, much of whose work is set in Mexico. The granddaughter of generals who rose to fame during the Mexican Revolution—her maternal grandfather, General Arnulfo R. Gomez, was running for the presidency of Mexico when he was executed in 1927 and is the subject of Martin Luis Guzmán's novel La sombra del caudillo *(1928)—Fontes explores Mexico's rich history, its many regions, and its ethnic and economic divisions. Positioning the United States as an absent other in her fiction, Fontes implicitly highlights its (dis)continuities with Mexico. Her first novel presents an unembroidered and rather naturalistic depiction of life on the Texas-Mexico border from the perspective of those who live on its southern side. In her second novel she takes her readers on a journey from Sonora to the Yucatán and on to Arizona during the time of the Porfiriato.*

Fontes was born in Laredo, Texas, but moved to Los Angeles to live with her maternal grandmother when she was nine years old. She received her BA and an MA in Comparative Literature with emphasis on Russian Literature from California State University, Los Angeles. Fontes is the author of two novels, First Confession *(1991) and* Dreams of the Centaur *(1996), the latter of which won the American Book*

Award for Fiction from the Before Columbus Foundation in 1997 and eloquently captures the Yaqui Indians' resistance against the Díaz regime. She is currently at work on the third part of the trilogy, The General's Widow. *Fontes has been the recipient of several National Endowment for the Humanities grants and a Carnegie-Mellon grant. She teaches English and Journalism at a Los Angeles High School, where she encounters students who speak almost one hundred different languages.*

In this interview, Fontes discusses the legacy of her Mexican ancestors and the impact of studying Russian literature on her writing. Her family background led to her repeated fictional returns to different moments in Mexican history, and her studies in Russian literature opened her eyes to the similarities between the Russian and the Mexican social fabric. Attuned to both ethnic and class divisions, Fontes explains how she had to cross the borders from her own upper-middle-class background and fully immerse herself in Yaqui history and culture to write Dreams of the Centaur. *A native Spanish speaker, she further discusses her initial negative experiences with the English language, as well as the importance of heritage languages in general.*

We conducted the first part of this interview on the campus of Texas A&M University–Corpus Christi in January of 1999. Fontes kindly agreed to answer additional questions via e-mail in the fall of 2007.

EMJ: *When and how did you start writing?*
MF: I started as a child. I always wanted to write songs because I was growing up at a time when Mexican singers—Jorge Negrete and Pedro Infante—were really taking off, and we had maids that also sang. Singing was a very clear form of expressing emotions beautifully, so I thought. My mother was a poet as well as a poetry reader, and she would teach me how songs are poems. So when I wasn't achieving in school, she said, "Write a poem before you can come in the house." Some people said, "That's so sadistic," but it really wasn't. I didn't feel unsure of myself, and I always knew that she was going to accept anything as long as it was written because I did not like to literally write on a piece of paper. I didn't know that she was keeping my stuff—it's in English and Spanish—until she mailed my writing in to a poetry contest when I was in fifth grade, and that was when I was first published. I remember holding a book, and it had my poem called "My Seashell," and it had something like an a-a-b-b-c-c rhyme scheme, but most importantly it was written in English.

Back then I would write mainly to myself. But when I had a near-death experience on the Rocky Mountains on the Western Slopes, and I was literally hanging from a twelve-thousand-foot cliff, I said to myself, "I haven't done it. I haven't written the books that I wanted to write." I had done some pseudonymous writing and I had sold some ideas for screenplays, but I'm talking about the stuff that you pull out of your *kischkas*, out of your inner self, I hadn't gotten around to doing it. I came back that summer in 1980 determined to do that and started writing. My education had nothing to do with it. It was a matter of urgency. I had to tell the story of Victor in *First Confession*. I had to tell the story of the great love a mother can have for her son in *Dreams of the Centaur*, and now I have to tell the story of how a woman refuses to be defeated, which is the story of my grandmother, and she's the parent that I choose to claim. You know, there are my biological parents, and I love them dearly, but the person who's *my* parent is my maternal grandmother.

EMJ: *You've said that you're working on a trilogy. Is the story of the woman who refuses to be defeated the third part of this trilogy?*

MF: Cormac McCarthy gave some really good advice; he said that when you say the word "trilogy," you start with the last book first. That way, if you don't finish it, you got it finished. So I knew I wanted to start with *First Confession*. That was the last part, and it ends in 1968 on purpose because that was the summer of the Mexican Olympics when the Mexican army turned itself loose on the Mexican students who were rebelling against the façade of Mexico. All those bodies were burnt and only sixty were reported dead, but hundreds of people disappeared. I self-exiled from Mexico at that moment in May of '68, just when that novel ends. Then I knew that the major research I was going to have to recreate had to do with the nineteenth century. Other than riding horses and shooting guns, I really didn't know anything about that, but then my research opened up to me the Yaqui plight. My family had really strong anti-Indian attitudes, and I was going to have to do that huge crossover and a lot of travel deep into Mexico for interviews because nothing was written. I had to get the Yaquis to talk about themselves. Now what I have to do is write the Hollywood story.

EMJ: *Does it have a working title?*

MF: *The General's Widow.* It takes place in Los Angeles, California, 1929 to 1939, during the Depression years. The title refers to my grandmother and her struggles after her husband was executed in 1927. He was running for

President of the Republic, and our lives were shadowed by his death. Remember the character Hector [from *Dreams of the Centaur*]? Well my grandfather, General Arnulfo Gomez, was like that young Hector; he taught at West Point here in the U.S. He's the only person or the first person in North America to receive the French Legion of Honor, a big award, and he was executed while he rose against the [Mexican] federal government for betraying the revolution. My grandmother's property and land were confiscated. But since she was a female, she had no legal rights. So she said, "I will never go back to Mexico. It is not a place for women," and she never did. She said, "Promise me that no matter what happens, you'll never marry a Mexican. But the main thing is that you get a college education. And get it *here* [in the United States]." I did that, and so this is her story. She started a Mexican restaurant in 1929, a month before the crash, the Great Depression. She survived because Cecil B. DeMille and a lot of the young upcoming movie moguls chose her Mexican little hole-in-the-wall as a place where they could talk business. It became an "in," kitschy type of place to go talk. We had that restaurant from 1929 to 1967. It still exists; it's a taco and tequila bar now, but the family got out of it. It's damn hard writing about the city you live in. I am fictionalizing many parts as I want to give grandmother a great sex life.

EMJ: *You earned an MA in Russian literature. Has that been at all influential on your writing?*
MF: Russian Realism, Gogol, Dostoyevsky—I've seen the parallels. I sort of felt them, but then I read an essay by Carson McCullers and really saw the parallels between Russian literature and Southern society with its very gender-defined behavior: this is what women do; this is what men do. There is the caste system which goes down to serfdom, a blind adherence to religion, a very strong division between what I profess to believe religiously and what I feel I can do in the world. And I said, "Gee, that is not only for Russians and for Southerners, it's also Mexicans, especially in the Mexico I know." I come from a Mexican middle-class family. Yes, we have a gender-defined and a caste system. I still believe we have serfs in Mexico, and this is 1999! I believe in the revolution of the Zapatistas, and I believe that we have to spill a lot more blood before it ends. I definitely believe that my writing gets its energy from that. Russian literature gave me access to the Russian struggle. World War I was starting, and they were still passing ordinances that finally got rid of serfdom in 1914 in Russia. I mean the parallels between Mexico and Russia

are shocking. I am very much involved with Mexican politics. My family is involved in Mexican politics. So I do go down there not to observe and write about it, but literally to get involved.

EMJ: *You have called yourself a Chicana. How do you see the relationship between yourself and the Chicana movement? Is there a tradition in Chicana literature as you see it?*

MF: I think it's still becoming. I was not a part of it because I was very much involved in the Black Revolution, simply because I was in Watts. Angela Davis was a teacher of mine. I was involved with the Free Rochelle McGee Committee. I was investigated by the FBI. I was also part of a huge system at the San Fernando rally getting the women to go out and register voters. But there my sister and I were reduced to gophers by these guys who were ten years younger than we were. By the blacks, at least we were treated equal.

But Chicano literature has really started to gain a tremendous momentum, and it's a wake-up call. We've had leaders who were in on it from the trenches—Cherríe Moraga, Ana Castillo, all of these, and they are people who write in so many venues. We have translators, like Norma Cantú, who's a tremendous translator and also a tremendous folklorist. I don't know as much as they do. I was not part of this. I always went to Anglo private schools. If there were other Latinas, they were the Somoza grandchildren. But I've been instructed by people like Norma Cantú and Ana Castillo and María Elena Gaitán, who is a comedian, and Gronk, a painter, and the Chicano professors at Cal State. They give me this and that to read, so I'm going through volumes of stuff.

EMJ: *You've talked about working on the first part of the trilogy, but you're also working on a libretto right now. What is it about?*

MF: I was approached by Joseph Julián González, who is a composer, to write a libretto, and all those songs that I was writing as a kid, all the operas my mom was playing and singing, came in handy. I come from an opera-loving family. My grandmother loved opera. She called her restaurant Carmen; she called her daughter Aida; she adopted a girl and called her Marta; she called my nephew Pucci, short for Puccini. So I don't have any trouble coming up with the libretto. The only problem is that the novelist in me is in conflict with the libretto, because the libretto has to be very simple, and the novelist in me wants to add this and that because it symbolizes something or other, but Joseph, the composer, says, no way. The opera is another avenue of getting out stuff that I know. Again it goes back to history. This is the 150th anniversary of the Mexican-American War, where Mexico lost two-fifths of its territory. Polk ran on a very simple expansionist platform: Texas, south to the Rio Grande, which is the Rio Bravo to us, and west to the Pacific. And Polk got it. In a period of two years, Mexico had eight presidents. Mexico had existed as a country only since 1821, so to go to war in 1846 was ludicrous. Everyone was a general or a serf; there was nothing in between. I found out that Tom Beringer is coming out with the St. Patrick's Battalion story, or Los San Patricios, this month or next, and he's playing the part of John Riley. There were Irish and German Catholics fighting [on the Mexican side in the war], one Pole, and a couple of Italians, but they were all Catholics; that was the main point. And writer [Michael] Hogan, an Irish Catholic, has shown that at first they were just treated as traitors, and he said no, that they were Catholics who arrived during the second American Great Revival, that's why they were called "foreign-born," which meant that they could be treated as less than slaves. They found a letter from one colonel to the lieutenant, which says, "Don't worry about the foreign-born; they weren't paid for." The question was what to do with the slaves, and what should the army do with the "foreign-born." The slaves were to be fed, but the army should not worry about the "foreign-born." They weren't paid for; in other words, they were less than slaves. And the reason for that was their Catholicism.

EMJ: *How so?*
MF: Because what Americans of the 1840s feared and loathed during a revival movement of the Puritan ethic were the Papists, the followers of Rome. Many Catholics, including my composer, don't know what Papists are, and I said, "Joseph, you don't believe in abortion. You don't believe in divorce. You're a Papist." So they were very afraid that Mexico, this huge papist power, would be at its back. They could see that the war between the states was coming, and Mexico would not be the first to abandon slavery—look at what they were doing to the Indians! At this time, three-fourths of the Mexican army was comprised of Indian tribes.

So the "foreign-born" couldn't bring themselves to loot the Catholic churches. There were two kinds of volunteers: they were either against the papists or they came to loot the papist gold from the churches. A lot of fortunes were made. The "foreign-born," the Irish and German Catholics, defected to Mexico, and they were offered 320 acres, women if they wanted them, and a salary; also, they could drink. The Irish and the Germans were not allowed to drink in the [U.S.] army, which was, given their cultures, a very serious restriction.

EMJ: *One reviewer said about your first published novel,* First Confession, *that the story "portrays the magic, passion, and innocence of childhood,"[1] whereas I rather got the impression that the novel is a stark demystification of the beauty and romance of childhood.*

MF: I was talking a bit about that this morning, how fearful I was during the Korean War. People would tell me that over those nearby mountains was Korea, and the Communists would come and kill you. I see childhood as probably one of the most *violent* periods of our lives, even without anything happening to us. But the fears are boundless, and the anger! As a mother you know that if any of your children at age three or four had been physically capable of acting out during a period of rage, you and your husband would be dead! There wouldn't be anything standing, and so what we do is basically train our children to be civilized. I don't believe in the goodness of childhood. I believe that children become good when we teach them guilt. What Andrea had as a character, and I think that's a gift that my father had, was the ability to act on her own desires; she had the ability not to feel guilty, to not act on her guilt if she felt it. And my dad brought me up that way. My mother tried to be a better conscience for me. Maybe the problem goes back to bullfighting, which was an integral part of my life as a child, causing me to view life guiltlessly. My father did teach me that God is an egg. He was very worried that I had gone to Catholic schools because he had gone to Catholic schools in Spain, where everything was a sin. He was beaten, and he knew the nuns were beating me, and he would force my mother to go to school with me because otherwise I'd run home. Childhood is not romantic; I think it is a naturalistic period. It's raw; it's survival of the fittest.

EMJ: *In the novel* First Confession *you portray two upper-middle-class children's initiation into life and society. Victor and Andrea learn about lives that are vastly different from theirs, the lives of the people who live on the river that runs along the Mexico-U.S. border. They're warned not to go to the river—bad things happen by the river, a whole different class of people live on the river. However, the lives of the people who live there touch those of the children and become interwoven very dramatically.*

MF: In real life what happened was that I used to go down to the river in the tractor my dad had bought me. For the novel, I had to find some kind of objective correlative, an extended metaphor that talked about the division in the two areas. I believe we are all divided, that we have a shadow self, the *Doppelgänger,* and the other self, the personality, in essence. The river served as the river Styx to foreshadow Victor's demise. There was the three-headed dog, the way the man is doing that torture—I hated writing that. The river also marks the divisions between the two cultures. As a kid, that was the one area where I was not allowed to go because children fell into that river all the time and they would drown, so my father said, "No!" He brought me home with the belt, spanking me when I went. He caught me because I wore a red and white baseball cap and when he was driving over the river, he'd say, "There she is." And I turned around, saw him, and, oh my god, he just went wild on me. So the river is both a symbol of death, a foreshadowing of death, and the Gorki-like lower depths that these children must see. It affects how they react to it; it affects who survives in life. Andrea is thrilled by it. She says, "Everything can happen there," and Victor agrees with her, but he doesn't want to go there and runs away while she stays. And she wants to go back. Here are two different points of view. When they find the town hooker, Andrea feels an affinity for the woman and says, "This money is hers [the hooker's]," but he says it's not hers because she was doing bad things to get it. They see the same thing and come up with two different solutions. Andrea wants to go back to the river, she wants to search for the treasure down there. Victor wants to steal the money, thinking it's safe because the woman can't do anything about it. That's just two different ways of looking at it. None of this happened, except for the death of Manolete [the Spanish bullfighter], but the river and the hooker offered a way for me to explore these dialectics.

EMJ: *How is Andrea's development shaped by her life on the border and between cultures? She also moves to L.A. and has an American mother and grandmother.*

MF: Yes, she's shaped by going to Hollywood, where everything is possible. Whatever you're not, you can invent. The big sex symbol at the time was Paulette Goddard, and so her grandmother shows up and has changed her name from Paula to Paulette. At the time, I was reading Bertrand Russell's thoughts about Saint Paul and the invention of Christianity. I was working with the idea of Paul and Paulette. Of course the grandmother says, "You can do anything you want to do" and then cuts her braids; this is a big step. Andrea is looking at all the female figures in her life. There's Candelaria [the maid], and there are all these other people, but the only person who offers her a door is Paulette. Of course by this time Armida, the hooker, is dead, and Victor is gone.

EMJ: *Candelaria also seems to be an important character; she's called a bruja, and there is an interesting relation between the maids and the children. What do the children learn from them?*

MF: Within the maid system, just like within the serf system, there are several classes—Petra is a maid, but she is actually the spine. As her name implies, she's the rock of the house. Candelaria lives independently of the fact that she's a maid—"I don't need your money; I don't need anything. I exist because of everything that has happened to me." She was a real person; she came into my family's life when I was in high school, and I brought her back into this because I needed Andrea to have someone to look at. Also, a lot of people misread Diane, Andrea's mother, as a weak character; she's not. Can you imagine not being able to speak Spanish? As her name implies, she's a moon person, Diana, and that in a country that worships the sun. So she's an outsider, the goddess of the moon living in the land of the Aztec sun. She has absolutely no say, and her husband can come and go. She was a totally reactive person.

EMJ: *Andrea and her mother have a love-hate relationship, and strained mother-daughter relations are explored in much literature written by women.*

MF: How do you love your mother when you know she's a victim? Victims are very difficult to love. I see this a lot in Chicana literature, that the woman first has to mend the rupture between herself and her mother, and all of us, several Chicana writers, have had to take that leap and reach back to the grandmother. The grandmother is really important to a lot of Chicana writers I know, without getting into their personal biographies or disclosing them. We have sat up talking and wondering what it is that we can find in our grandmothers that we don't in our mothers. And I've talked to my mom about it, but of course she was raised in the United States; she even had to relearn how to speak Spanish.

EMJ: *You gave a talk at Stetson University on the theology of the novel, and of course religion figures prominently in* First Confession. *The title implies a cleansing, and, as one reviewer² said, this is the children's time to be bad before they have to be good. How would you describe the role of theology in the novel?*

MF: It has to do with guilt and expiation, and the fact that there's a built-in safety net—so long as I can confess it, so long as I can do penance for it, basically I have permission to do it again. What I did at Stetson was field student questions, and the questions they asked me the most were, first of all, was Andrea autobiographical? I said no, I was a lot worse. Truly—but I had to clean her up for fiction, otherwise people weren't going to believe this. And number two, did I like her? I said I liked her once Victor leaves and she's on her own and then goes back up to spy on Armida. Then I really start to like her. As long as she's with Victor, she's still split; she's not being loyal to herself. Originally the novel ended with the first communion, which is where the film is going to end. But the epilogue is really what prompted my writing it because it's after my own friend Victor's suicide that my life hit a wall and I had nothing, and the way I healed myself was only by doing that Intensive Journal.³ Every single one of those early entries ended up with Victor. In one of the journal entries in the Ira Progroff Journal, I found Andrea's voice. I accessed that voice that had been dormant since I was a kid and ah, it just came up. I went home so I wouldn't lose the melody of it and put it down and then continued, and even now when I go back to write the film—I'm not having a voice-over because it's considered passé to have a voice-over in film—I still have to go deep into my head to find her voice again.

EMJ: *You said that this is the story of Victor, whereas to me nine-year-old Andrea was in the foreground because she is such an interesting and unusual female character, not only* pushing *the limits of acceptable behavior but clearly transgressing them; she's so insistent on pursuing her own ideas and meddling with other people's affairs.*

MF: To me it's the story of Victor. That's what I'm doing, I'm healing myself by writing about Victor, and I refused to change his name. Now when does Victor earn his name? Victor earns his name when he chooses to commit suicide and he bypasses the Catholic Church. It's in his suicide note. The original note was five pages long, but I had to boil it down. It's a whole series of imperative sentences. It's all been boiled down. If I have to think of a piece of mine, anything that I've written in fiction or nonfiction, I think that suicide note is the most tightly structured piece of writing. There isn't one cognate in there that linguistically does not contain the body of it. Some of us are cast, and he says, "cast so solidly that the slightest breach would snap," and then I realized that Victor was cast that way, and that was probably the reason that I needed him so much in my life, because I'm a very unbridled person. I agree with you, I'm writing about Andrea, but in order for me to write about Andrea I had to go *through* Victor. He was that conscience, and it's his inability to bend. Andrea is very proud of her ability to keep secrets, but it turned out that he's the one who really keeps secrets, and those secrets killed him. I always felt very betrayed by him. My mom told me that he died in a car accident, but my intuition about him was right. Here I was in my thirties, and my mom tells me this nonsense.

EMJ: *Alejo, in* Dreams of the Centaur, *is also a teenager who has to grow up before his age because of his father's death. Now that you say that it's a trilogy, I see the continuity in your use of the last name Durcal. The novel reminds me of* One Hundred Years of Solitude, *not just because it's a family chronicle, but also because Felipa as a character is so much like Ursula. She has incredible strength. What this woman is able to do!*
MF: She lived to 103.

EMJ: *Again in this novel you delve into the past, and your concern with Mexican history is what makes your writing distinctive. You take your U.S. American audience to Mexico and through the country. Another talk you gave in San Antonio last year was entitled "Unburying Lost History." Where does your interest in history come from? You did extensive research for* Dreams of the Centaur. *How did this interest develop?*
MF: I think it started with my parents talking at the dinner table and the fact that my mother would always blame my father. My mother is about ten years younger than my dad. When she fell in love with him she was about seven and he was seventeen, or she was ten and he was nineteen or something like that. She always said, "When I grow up I'm going to marry you," and he said, "Yeah." Then later she always used to say, "But *your* dad took the money and ran, and *my* dad stayed and fought." And I thought, here we go, it's going to be one of those lunches or dinners. These were both children of political and military celebrities. They'd traveled as young children under

pseudonyms because they were afraid of being kidnapped. They were child celebrities. As many children of famous people, they had no lives of their own—they'd always be talking about that.

So history has never been dead for me, and I was always raised to remember that we are part of the Fontes and Gomez; we are part of history and we make history; we don't know how, but as my father said, "If you don't believe in something, then get up and fight it." My mother was an artist in the thirties, and she joined the Young Communist League and a whole group of intellectuals. During the McCarthy period in the fifties, she was exiled, which is a novel after *The General's Widow* down the line [laughs]—we do things; we act. I've not been brought up in my life any other way.

Also, my parents were real history buffs and their children knew all about the French, Spanish, Russian, and all the other revolutions before we were out of grade school. I don't think you know who you are if you don't know your history. That's a tad un-existential, but I have learned this to be true. I think Mexicans need to know about the Yaqui enslavement; Mexico has always denied having slavery, and there I was in Sonora speaking with Yaquis whose parents had been born slaves.

Alejo in real life was fourteen. Again, they said, "Sorry, no no no, make him sixteen." I finished the book, and the boy was still a virgin. I was teaching Chicana literature and said, "Guys, I finished my novel, but the guy's unlaid." "Oh, no, no, Ms. Fontes, you've got to give him a sex life." So I said, "Okay, you guys help me write the sex life." So my sixth-period Chicano students would discuss how he should lose his virginity. All the guys came up with six plans. But well, it has to take place on the table; his father was laid out on the table, his father *made* the table. But they said it should be a wall job, not a table job, but his leg was amputated on a table. As a woodworker I made tables, so they said okay, a table. So my students helped me. I had left his sex life out because I had gotten so tangled up with everything else. And it just took about a week and the sex life was there.

EMJ: *As I said earlier, I think Felipa is also an incredibly strong character.*
MF: She was also in real life. I didn't include half of the stuff that this woman did.

EMJ: *She literally sawed off and amputated her son's leg, followed him into battle, and then took him to Arizona?*

MF: She actually did that. She amputated it on the battlefield. The doctor, Doctor Lowe, said he could not direct me how she did it. They knew that she sliced and cauterized. What I did not want to do was to write a cheater scene: "She picked up the saw . . . ," and then two weeks later have the kid continue with his life. I really had to learn how to amputate.

EMJ: *What is the origin of her strength? There's a statement Felipa's tía Mercedes makes that "No chino will help you . . . Not against Mexican women in Mexico."[4] Both Mercedes and Felipa very much contradict popular depictions of Mexican women as submissive and subservient.*

MF: I've never seen Mexican women like that! I've never seen them among our maids—who the hell handles all those machos? You never read the African American women depicted that way. I remember my mother standing up to my dad when my father would demand the money for our school tuition because he was in a hot domino game and had a winning streak, and my mother would hide the tuition money between towels, the last place where he would look for it. Truly, I don't experience Mexican women as submissive. Now are we talking about the woman who is selling chiclets with three kids and she's pregnant—that's poverty, and that's a violent image, because poverty is violence. A lot of people have been shocked to be approached in Dublin by a redhead with rotten teeth and three kids, begging. They have never seen redheads with beautiful freckles begging. It's a wipe-out. That's poverty. I have a problem with my high-school girls when they get pregnant. "Miss," they say, "you can't help it when they want sex, you can't help it." And I say, "You get pregnant now at sixteen, you're going to be really pissed at twenty-two. The number one killer of children is their biological mother, now you think about that." I chose years ago not to breed because my grandmother always said, "One day you're going to get yours," and I was scared to death, and so I never bred. I'm the great-aunt. All of my sisters' and brothers' kids run away to my house, and I teach them three things: how to drive, how to tend bar, and how to play poker. A lot of them live with me; there's always a place for them. But I don't experience Mexican women as submissive. Who said that? I don't know where that comes from.

EMJ: *One thing that tends to shock readers of* Dreams of the Centaur *is the blunt language you use, the descriptions of the physical functions and of violence. Is that to recreate the harshness of the Yaqui experience?*

MF: That's just the way I write, and spending time on a ranch, and seeing the fact that, damn, it's hard to be an animal and to be a rancher. People have no idea how hard it is to work a ranch. I spent a lot of summers there, and I've been literally resewn back together [points out several scars]. The blunt imagery is there because it's real. None of it is artificial; if anything, I tamed it. I told students some of the things I left out out of respect for the Yaqui, specifically the Yaqui women, who were violated in the worst possible way.

EMJ: *One of the ideas running through the novel is freedom and its opposite, a topic that is often explored in American literature. Is Alejo a free agent when killing his father's murderer? Is freedom illusory?*
MF: He is bound, just like my real uncle Alejo. He had no choice.

EMJ: *Bound by the society's honor code?*
MF: Like his defense attorney said, "Alejo did no more than you would expect your sons to do for you had you been murdered." Alejo wrote poetry when he was in prison, and some of it exists; some of it my mom had. He wished that he had been born a woman so that he could be important to his mother, but he knew he'd be forced to kill this man. And he knew that he'd inflict upon his mother her greatest pain. He actually wrote lines of poetry, "Why didn't the Virgin Mary make me a woman so I could console my mother?" He knew ahead of time that he was going to be the source of her greatest pain. He only lived until he was thirty-three; he literally drank himself to death. Once my General Hector's life took off on its road to success, he let himself go. He never got over the amputation; there was no such thing as therapy or whatever, and he didn't have a woman to take care of him. We'll never know if he had any children. He did send the general a ring and a ring for my mother, and she has some of the poetry that he wrote, but other than that we know very little of his personal life. He ran a barber shop in real life, but that's too unromantic. So I made him a horse breeder in the novel. They stored guns and ran them into Mexico for the revolution, and he took part in that. Now the general, my grandfather, never touched alcohol, neither did my other grandfather, and they both were sons of drinkers! But they were great womanizers. There was an old five-peso bill with a very pretty gypsy woman on it, and she was a twin. These twins were mistresses of both my grandfathers, and that's how they got their pictures on the five-peso bill.

EMJ: *The issue of freedom returns at the end of the battle when the Yaquis decide to jump off the mountaintop. Is death, then, better than imprisonment?*
MF: Yes, Mazocoba was a big military secret. They pulled all the Mexican troops out of Baja California and brought them all back to Sonora. They brought the soldiers up there and circled the Yaquis. This was in the year 1900, in January. The attitude was, this is a new century, let's get rid of them. They told the Mexican plebeian soldiers, "You will go up there or we will shoot you, and you will bring the Yaquis down." The Mountain Yaquis had already decided. They were betrayed by Pluma Blanca, who sold the secret access for some bars on a shirt, and the Yaquis did choose death. The ones who were captured were sent to Yucatán. Charco, a fictional character, who is a half-breed will be one of the generals who goes there since the Yaqui battalion wanted no Mexicans to go with them as they ride back to Yucatán. That'll be in *The General's Widow*. Charco will tell it; it's all in a flashback, and he'll tell it. He wanted no Mexicans to ride with them. So they went down there and freed the Yaquis. A lot of them walked back. The Yaqui has never surrendered, never signed a peace treaty. That's one of the reasons they're outsiders among a lot of the native tribes in Mexico. The Mayo from Sonora, the Pima, they all signed treaties. The Yaquis are like the New Zealand Maoris or the Florida Seminoles, they never surrendered.

EMJ: *In the middle of the novel you do something that creative writing students are told is a definite no-no. You go from third-person narration to first-person and back to third. Is that to depict Alejo's estrangement from himself?*
MF: It's to place the reader right there in the present tense and to create an awareness that this is unfolding right in front of *me*. And I didn't know how the reader was going to react, so it was an experiment. You just can't sustain it very long, though.

EMJ: *This is also the part where Alejo seems to confront his dark side; he himself commits all the atrocities on the Yaqui women and the rest of the prisoners.*
MF: And that's foreshadowed when he goes to break Moro and he spits out the Yaqui crucifix. That's a symbol that remains unexplained, but if anybody delves into Yaqui cosmology, they'll understand why that happens. This is something that took me three Easter ceremonies to learn about, to get the Yaquis to talk to me about. They tell you things very reluctantly. I went back to check everything. The hanging of the Yaqui mothers, for example, I didn't

put in there because I knew it would scar survivors. When a Yaqui woman has been raped, she is no longer part of the tribe among the Yaqui purists, so I also left that out, as well as the forced breeding and the suicide pacts among Yaqui women: I bite your jugular and you bite mine.

EMJ: *The novel, with its two courtroom scenes that depict Alamo's social structure, and then Alejo's travels through Mexico, seems to explore the state of the nation during the Porfiriato, a multicultural society at war with parts of itself.*
MF: Yes, people don't understand the complexity of Mexican society, which is very much like Spanish or German society. It's a series of multiples. These people were roped into becoming a country; the country itself didn't exist, so that's what that's about.

NS: *Could you talk about your early experiences with language? Was it difficult to keep up with your Spanish? What were your first encounters with English?*
MF: My early experiences with the language took place at the Ursuline Academy in Laredo on the Tex-Mex border. My parents and their friends were bilingual and I heard them speak, but I didn't pay attention. I had no desire to learn English. My friends and I spoke only Spanish and that seemed to be all right, despite my parents' desire for me to adopt English. I spent *three* years in first grade as I couldn't pass the test for English, and the nuns were adamant that only those who passed were promoted. I had no shame about flunking as I had a permissive father. So my language was Spanish and then when I was ten, I adopted English.

EMJ: *You mentioned earlier that your initial associations with English were bad ones and that Ursuline nuns hung you by your braids and made you pronounce your name in English. You said that you thought that something inside of you would die when you spoke English. Could you tell us the story?*
MF: These were not the nuns that tied me by my braids; those were the Holy Name Sisters when I was ten years old and was in boarding school in Los Angeles. My parents resorted to a full-time boarding school so I would have to speak English, and that was where a nun tied me by my braids to the chains of a swing. They also wanted me to pronounce my name in English, which is ludicrous: how do you pronounce "Montserrat" in English? Because of all this discipline, my first experiences with English were negative. The

only good experiences I had at the Alhambra Convent of the Holy Name Sisters were riding horses. But, by the end of the first year at the convent, I was an English-speaking student. My Spanish never left me. My fears were that I would not be able to sing the corridos I loved so much, but I learned that I could continue to sing them. That was when I was sure I was going to die. I associated my first language with my Self, and changing my language meant changing my Self.

NS: *Do you find that your students are still discouraged from speaking their home languages? Now is there more of an awareness of the benefits of multilingualism?*

MF: I find that among my Latino students the division is about seventy-thirty, with the majority of Spanish-speaking students keeping their language. Second- and third-generation Latinos are more willing to let their Spanish language fall by the wayside. Still, our classes for Spanish-speaking students are full as some of them see the benefits of bilingualism. I teach at a ninety-plus minority school—with most of the students being Mexican and the rest Central American.

NS: *You articulate the connections among language, identity, and social attitudes, in particular in* Dreams of the Centaur. *For example, Felipa forbade her son to learn Yaqui, the language of the Indians she feared and despised. How important is the maintenance of heritage languages, especially those spoken by communities under pressure to assimilate to the majority language and culture, for example Spanish in the U.S. and Indian languages in Mexico?*

MF: I think that our heritage language is vital to our identity. It was for me. With different languages come different mores. A simple example is when I started to speak English, I was more willing to consider cutting off my braids and wearing lipstick. That was an acceptable American custom. "Good" Mexican girls did not do that until they were fifteen.

As for Indian languages in Mexico, Spanish is not the main language in the country. People still belong to their gente, or tribe. They still have a cacique, or tribe leader; they learn Spanish in school or out in society. Many Yaquis today refuse to speak Spanish. Oaxaca has multiple Indian dialects, as does Yucatán. Native peoples in Mexico keep their language. In Los Angeles, we have a Zapotec Center.

NS: *You don't code-switch or use many Spanish phrases in your writing. Do you do this with your English-speaking audience or your editors in mind?*
MF: I don't think of code-switching when I'm writing. My concern is clarity. When Spanish serves me better, I use it, if not, I stay with English. It's not really in my head.

NS: *Who do you consider your primary audience?*
MF: I don't know who my primary audience is. I like to think it is someone like me, someone who is bicultural or people who are interested in a culture beyond theirs. Chicanas read my work, but I have several Anglo readers who read my books in college, and their interest is genuine. Anglo teachers use my works in universities in Modern Literature classes; I hope my work is not ghettoized; that would hurt me. I like to think of my messages as being universal.

SELECTED WORKS BY MONTSERRAT FONTES

Novels
Dreams of the Centaur. New York: W. W. Norton, 1996.
First Confession. New York: W. W. Norton, 1991.

NOTES

1. Johanna M. Burkhardt, "First Confession," *Library Journal* 115, no. 21 (1990): 162.
2. Ibid., 162.
3. Psychologist Ira Progroff developed the Intensive Journal Method that uses writing as a tool for self-growth.
4. *Dreams of the Centaur.* (New York: W. W. Norton, 1996), 131.

Diana Montejano, © Olan Mills

BRAIDING LANGUAGES, WEAVING CULTURES

Conversation with Diana Montejano

The work of poet, activist, and educator Diana Montejano originates from and is representative of the confluence of languages and cultures in the U.S.-Mexico borderlands. From the perspective of a bilingual and bicultural writer, she describes here "one Chicana's enduring love affair with poesia and the art of expression."[1] As an educator in San Antonio, Texas, she is invested in encouraging her students to make connections to their cultures, histories, and languages. She shares with them her insight that an awareness of the discontinuities of life in the borderlands—the Catholicism, the educational system, the physical and psychological mestizaje, patriarchal dominance, and gender roles—may serve as the springboard for their writing and lead to better self-expression and increased interpersonal understanding.

Montejano is a native of Del Rio, Texas. She received her BA in Communication Arts from the University of the Incarnate Word in San Antonio, Texas, and holds an MFA in Creative Writing from the University of Texas–El Paso. She worked as a legislative research aide to State Senator Joe J. Bernal, one of the cosponsors of the state's first Bilingual Education Bill, served as interviewer for the

National Council of La Raza, was active in the Crystal City I.S.D. and Lanier High School "walkouts," which protested the lack of educational opportunities for Chicanos/as, and was one of the original volunteers for the Southwest Voter Education and Registration Project. She currently teaches English and Creative Writing to at-risk youth in San Antonio. Her publications include the chapbook Nebulous Thoughts (1997) as well as individual poems in The Virgin of Guadalupe, The Rio Grande Review, and Blue Mesa Review. In 1996, an excerpt of her poem "El honor" was published in The Chronicle of Higher Education. Her most recent work, the short story "First Crossing," was published by the Xicano/a Education Project Anthology, Desaógate (2005).

In this interview, which took place in October 1999 when she visited the campus of Texas A&M University–Corpus Christi for a reading and book signing, Montejano highlights the importance of interethnic alliances in her quest to become a writer, tracing her beginnings to her reading of the voices of resistance in the African American Civil Rights Movement and her subsequent turn to Chicanos and Chicanas for mentorship. These alliances led her to view Mexican Americans in the United States from a pan-hemispheric perspective: "somos de las Américas," she says. She further comments on bilingualism, the politics of language in the borderlands, and her technique of "braiding" English and Spanish in her poetry. As she says elsewhere, the freedom to express herself through poetry "came about through acquisition, through experimentation, and through a great deal of study."[2]

NS: *When did you become aware that you were a writer?*

DM: I think that I was fifteen years old. I had a nun who taught me, and I try to impress this on my students, it took *one* teacher. I was the scourge of school. I was a lot of trouble, and I acknowledge that now; at that time I would not acknowledge that I was any trouble at all. But I was a natural rebel. Part of that rebellion was speaking Spanish because at that time Spanish was totally forbidden. One of the weird things was that the school set up a court of your peers to judge you on your infractions, breaking the rules and stuff like that. Every Friday they would take these students before court, and they had their judges and their panel. Of course we didn't have defense lawyers. You were just up there, and, "Today you did this, on this day you did that," and they had their little snitches posted all around the school. This was horrible.

NS: *And speaking Spanish was one of the infractions?*

DM: Speaking Spanish was one of the infractions. What made it worse was my brother, my big brother, was one of the judges. I think it was done on purpose; it was a continual pattern. My younger brother and I were always there at the court, and of course big brother would go home and start saying, "Look, they're embarrassing me, and I'm in this position," and we told him, "You sell-out!" Having my brother there added to my anger. In high school, I met an Irish nun who went and told the principal that punishing me was not working. "It seems like she thrives on this punishment," she said. She wanted to take charge of me, and so every day after school I would go to Sister Sabina. She told me one day, "Diana,"—she was the only nun that did not change my name from "Diana" [Spanish pronunciation] to "Diana" [English pronunciation], which is a problem that I have even with Chicanos or Latinos—and she says, "Diana, punishing you in the normal way doesn't work with you. I'm not here to punish you, I'm here to guide you." I'm looking at her like, "Huh, why don't you just punish me, it's easier; put me to clean the bathrooms, wash the dishes or something," but she gave me a book, J. D. Salinger's *Catcher in the Rye*. And she goes, "Well, if you want to consider this your punishment, fine." She said, "Take your time, read the book."

I wondered, "What is this? What *is* this?" and I actually enjoyed it very much. Then she kept bringing me books, LeRoy Jones and Eldridge Cleaver. I read *The Autobiography of Malcolm X*. It was a banned book, and she brought it to me, a nun brought it to me! You know, they had those big habits and those big huge pockets, and she was digging in it and she was saying, "I didn't give this to you, but I want you to read it." Then she started bringing me poetry—Countee Cullen, Langston Hughes, Gwendolyn Brooks. When I read Gwendolyn Brooks, I wrote my first poem, "Crying." She saw it and started praising me, "You have a flair for writing. I'm not sure you're aware of this, but you have a flair for writing." So that was all I needed, and I started writing and writing and writing, and I wrote a book. I wrote a research paper on the voices of resistance of African American writers at that time. There was no Hispanic or Chicano literature to speak of. So a lot of my poetry was patterned after Countee Cullen, Gwendolyn Brooks, Langston Hughes, Richard Wright, Zora Neale Hurston—on and on the list went. I noticed how comfortable Zora Neale Hurston was with the black vernacular. I read that even her own people criticized her for making the blacks look like they're uneducated, and she responded by saying, "Well, I'm writing the way the people are, the way they speak," and it struck me; it definitely struck a chord. But at the same time my braiding didn't just take off then; I know this is the way we spoke in the barrio, the way we spoke at home. Dad spoke English, Mom spoke Spanish. This is how we learned to speak English and Spanish.

My mom learned English with us. She learned how to do her reading and writing by sitting down and doing the exact same lessons we were assigned to do. I went up to approximately the third grade before I really grasped what English was and what they were saying because I was so hung up in the "You're *not* going to teach me in it"—the whole rebellion thing. I think part of it was the anger at home because of the injustice that was going on. My parents could not buy a home in a certain section of town. All of this I'm listening to, I'm absorbing even though I'm not cognizant, I'm not fully aware of why, and what's going on.

NS: *Even in the third grade you were angry?*
DM: I was in the third grade. I was angry all throughout school, even college. It took me a long time; it took me a very long time to realize why I was angry. In third grade, they were trying to change my writing hand from left to right, and they were literally hitting me with a ruler, but sideways, which really hurt more.

NS: *So you were getting punished not only for the language that you're using, but for writing with your left hand too? It's amazing you became a writer.*
DM: Well, thanks to Sister Sabina and the fact that I saw her doing things that she was not really supposed to do, and that she would say, "It's okay, it's okay, you just need to take what you need from these books, what you can absorb, and realize that these experiences are not uniquely yours. There's a whole bunch of people out there that have experienced what you have." I wrote a play, "Jana," at that time, and it was patterned after a story about a daughter who was angry because she lacked a father-figure since her father was in prison. It first was a story, but I turned it into a play. I actually read it to my classmates, and that's where everything took off. Sister Sabina asked me to read it, and then she asked me to run for the school editor position. I was looking at her, "Are you sure you want me to do that?" And she said, "Yes, you have what it takes." And I said, "OK, I'll run."

I won by one vote because I had a bad reputation. I was being escorted to school by the police. I was playing hooky. How can you go play hooky in a brown uniform? That was pretty stupid of me. Everybody knew you were from Catholic school, but I thought I was being real cool.

"What's wrong with you?" That was a question I grew up with. "What's wrong with you?" It took me a long time, and I don't think that I started working out the answer until I got older, when I started that introspective period of my life where I was trying to figure out well, what *is* wrong with me? There's nothing wrong in the end. Or maybe just a few things wrong, but not as much as people had said, including my own mother. "What's wrong with you? Why can't you just do what they ask you to do? Behave. They don't want you to speak Spanish, well then, *don't* speak Spanish." And I said, "No, no, that's not what it's about!"

EMJ: *In Sandra Cisneros's "Bien Pretty," the narrator, Lupe, says that Spanish has certain associations for her that English does not. Do you also associate certain things with speaking Spanish and others with English?*
DM: I don't know. I think that I would tend to associate Spanish more with love and romanticism and music.

EMJ: *That's what she says. Spanish is the language of poetry, of passion.*
DM: It's all so rhythmic, lyrical. It's a lyrical language in contrast to English, which has some guttural context to it that makes it kind of harsh. Do I know what I understand in either English or Spanish? I can't tell you. What I think in Spanish or what I associate Spanish with is anger, all the emotions, I think. I can express myself pretty well in Spanish. When I'm in love, when I hate, when I'm disgusted, when I'm about to launch into some kind of rebellion, I take off. But it depends, again, on whom I am addressing here.

NS: *You said that earlier in your career you didn't realize that you could go back and forth from English to Spanish; you thought you had to write either in Spanish or in English. What made you decide that you could do both?*
DM: Back in 1981, I was sending all my poetry to Cecilio García-Carmarillo, I mean, poetry that I had written since I was fifteen, sixteen, seventeen. Cecilio was encouraging me at that time to mix, braid the two languages. He's a Chicano poet, former editor of the *Caracol.* He's a very, very well-known

figure in Chicano literature who lives in Albuquerque. He was an activist here in South Texas. He's originally from Laredo, and he went to UT [the University of Texas] at Austin. I met him through my big brother [historian David Montejano], and we became very good friends because I was a poet and so was he. And so he would compose all these poems, and he would do the braiding at that time while I would continue to stick either to all English or all Spanish. I'm not going to say that's the dividing line, but it wasn't until I reached the University of Texas–El Paso in 1993, when I actually started playing with mixing languages, the braiding, and I liked it. I met Ben Sáenz, who became my mentor and teacher, my sponsor at UTEP, and he encouraged me to experiment.

It's not code switching, a lot of people call it code switching. I'm not so sure it's code switching because I tend to think that code switching is still taking it a step further and mixing the slang. The slang words, like the "ramflas" and the "carcachas" and all this which stand for cars, and "chantes" and stuff like that, you just don't say if you're speaking to anyone. I wouldn't go and speak to my mother about my "chante" or my "ramfla," my "carucha," my "carcacha." I would just say "Quieres ir al carro, vamos para la casa." But let's say that I'd speak to someone who is streetwise, I would instantly know.

NS: *It depends on whom you're speaking to.*
DM: That's right. I tend to assess the situation very quickly, and I can't tell you how that process comes about.

NS: *So you call mixing Spanish and English "braiding"?*
DM: The good English and the good Spanish. In code switching, it's almost like the slang and the street lingo are mixed in with it. Like when I say, "hissy-fit. She's about to have a hissy-fit." That's something you just don't normally come out and say to a learned person; you would change the word. And so that's like an English slang, and I tend to pair them. I don't know why.

EMJ: *Do you do it for poetic purposes? Because it sounds better in your poetry?*
DM: I'll write the poem in whichever language it comes out. I'll write it, and when I go back to revise it, I start playing with the words. I really love it if they have what we call double entendres. There's a line that I wrote, "Pedacitos

you fed to gods, sin consciencia." "Pieces that you fed to gods without conscience." But that "sin," "without" in Spanish, also stands for "sin" in English.
So it kind of fits within the text about a young woman who lost her virginity
and her innocence, and that cut her up in pieces that "you fed to gods," and
that's a sin.

EMJ: *So it adds a layer of complexity.*
DM: Yes, it makes it a little bit more complex. I try to do stuff like this although sometimes I'm not very successful. Where do I stick in the English
and the Spanish? It usually comes out in my revision, and I do play around
a lot. Does this sound better? No. Does that sound better? And sometimes
I'll just say, "What the heck, this is what I wrote." Of course, in the revision
process, you start editing yourself, and sometimes you just leave it the way
it is, or you'll just take out the word and say, "Heck, the last lines came out
in Spanish."

I was trying to play with the César Chávez poem, "I Want to Die Like
You, César," to make it like a bilingual sestina. I was not so successful, and
I'd still like to go back and play with it—I know I am, because it's become a
challenge now.

NS: *Is this a new poem you wrote?*
DM: It's a new poem that I found. It was incomplete, and I was supposed
to send it off about three years ago. I found it, and I finished it, and I came
here and read it [at an earlier lecture]. The last lines, except for "in my sleep,"
or "laid with a gentle heart," are it for the English. It just took off in the
Spanish, and I left it that way. I did not go back to change anything because
I believe somewhere in the poem lies the translation. That's something else
I'm conscious of in my poetry: I want my audience to understand that if
they listen very carefully, they can pick up the context, the gist of the poem,
the meaning because there is nothing that I say wholly either in English or
Spanish, it's just braided so that you can understand.

EMJ: *Oftentimes when students in my sophomore literature survey classes read
a poem by Pat Mora or Sandra Cisneros, they very much resist the Spanish in it.
"I can't understand this. This is not a poem for me," they say. They immediately
back off and don't want to engage. How would you respond?*

DM: I have the same problem with my students now, and these are the street kids so you would think that they're rebels at heart and would embrace this, but it's not true. They say, "My parents never taught me Spanish." It happened in my own family. You have parents teaching children both Spanish and English, and you have parents who are just teaching them English because they don't want them to suffer or have experiences like I did. What do you say to them? I tell my students, "You know you need to be patient and try to learn this because you're going to love it." I gave this same poetry reading to my students prior to coming here, and they were mesmerized. Now these are the students that don't understand Spanish. They're Chicanos, they're Hispanos, and they say, "I don't understand the language." But I have some Anglo children there, I have some Black children there, and they were just mesmerized. I said, "If you listen very carefully, you're going to be able to understand what I'm saying because of the braiding." And I said "You just need to pick up on it and you're going to learn, but you do have to listen."

When we grow older, all of a sudden there's a big demand for bilingual this, bilingual that, and you're wondering, "What happened here? Where did we go wrong?" On the one hand they ostracized us for speaking Spanish when we were very little, and when we grow up, we totally convert to the other side, to English. But then you grow older and there's this demand. People look at you like, "Oh, are you bilingual, by the way?" You say, "No, I'm not, I really don't speak Spanish. I can understand it or I can read it," and they're looking at you like, "Well, what's wrong with you? Aren't you Chicana? Aren't you Hispana? You're supposed to know it; this is part of your culture." We've spent all of our formative years dealing with this system that says, "No you can't do it [speak Spanish]; you can't do this at this time."

NS: *Many of our students' parents were punished in school for speaking Spanish, so as children they weren't allowed to speak Spanish at home because their parents wanted them to "fit in" and to succeed in school. They say they're upset when people say, "Why can't you speak Spanish? You're Hispanic, aren't you?" Or they're upset that they can't talk to their grandparents who only speak Spanish. For the Hispanic population now in their twenties, the loss of a language has been a real tragedy.*

DM: It's amazing. In my home we could not visit my grandfather and utter a single word in English. "Okay" was about it, and it had to be "Okay"

[Spanish accented], not "Okay" [English accent]. He was one of those gung-ho ex-revolucionarios who served in World War I and was discriminated against. He was just a very angry man, angry at all the injustice. This was my mother's father, so my mother was angry too, though I think my father was angry as well. We children absorbed all of this. But you could not enter his home and speak English, even when we were in school and wanted to come in and impress him. I think that happened to my big brother once, and he said, "If you're going to speak that foreign language in my home, get out, go outside; foreigners belong outside my home." That was very harsh. He always looked like he was angry, and they tell me I have that same characteristic, that same look. "Miss, you look like you're always angry." And I say, "I'm *not* always angry."

One of the things that made me very angry was the fact that the nuns who were running the Catholic school had fled the Mexican Revolution—they were all Mexican nuns, and they all understood what you were saying. "¿Puedo ir al baño? Quiero ir al baño. Quiero ir hacer esto, o lo otro." They would sit there and pretend they didn't understand you, though they spoke only broken English. They had set up a system of spies in school as to who spoke Spanish and who didn't. I think they would have been perfect torturers. Yet my experience was that I found a good teacher, and that's all I needed. She believed in me, and she understood that I needed someone to believe in me.

The other thing is that the Spanish we were taught in Spanish class and that we were allowed to speak only there had to be Castilian Spanish. Who's going to speak this? "Cómo está usted?" [Castilian accent], and this is the Spanish we were expected to speak. It was really crazy.

We had Spanish class right after lunch, and Sister Augustine would come in—I wrote a poem about it—she would come in with her Castilian thing, and she would start spitting at us. [Laughter] All of us would have assigned seats, and we would say, "Oh, my god, here she comes." She never understood why all the front row would be gone. And of course I was always in the front because they had to watch me.

EMJ: *Do you think there's more room for voices like yours in the American mainstream today?*
DM: I think it's important. Listen, it's in advertising, and once it gets to advertising, everyone knows about it. "Yo quiero Taco Bell" and "mas food,

less dinero"—give me a break! It's acceptable once it finds its way into the mass media. These are national commercials that are broadcast all over the United States!

EMJ: *What about in publishing?*
DM: In publishing even more so. But are there publishers out there that are sensitized to this aspect, this experience? I don't know. I can't tell you. I was telling this student yesterday that Bilingual Press has a waiting list of at least two years. In other words, they'll take your work, but you have to wait two years until it's out. I don't know what Arte Público's wait list is. I think those are the only two major Latino publishing houses. There are no literary agents, no female literary agents that are Latina, neither Cubana nor Dominicana. It's just a rough business, and it's rough even if you speak all English. The young lady was talking about writing the traditional novel. What? Traditional novel in terms of all English? How would you put a Latino, Chicano experience in all English when a major portion of what you identify with is in Spanish?

That's another thing that leads me to anger. My grandfather always told me when I was old enough to understand, "You know Spanish isn't even our first language. You know you've got the Nahua." He started telling me things like "metate" and "tomate" and all these "ates." He said, "Those are Nahua derivatives." Of course he didn't tell me in that language. He says, "Primero eres India," first you're Indian and then you're everything else. If you're looking for an identity, primero eres India." And he would say in Spanish, "Unfortunately, all this has been taken away from us."

That's part of my own theory about why our youth are in trouble. They are because there's that sense of disconnectedness. We can blame the deterioration of the family, the family values, and the educational system, and on and on. But I believe that if you go back and start teaching them to be proud of what their origins are, it's not just the Spanish/European crap. I don't mean "crap" in a disrespectful way because the Europeans and the Spanish people brought us some good things, but most of it was bad. And so, we're still hanging on to this language of the conquerors, the conquest language, la idioma de la conquista, and that's what we know. That happened years and generations ago, and I was telling my students this: "You know you have the blood of royalty running through your veins. You don't even know it. We invented this, we did that, we performed brain surgeries on patients who survived—they have found the skulls. All this was going on thousands of years before Christ. Probably almost simultaneously with the Egyptians and the Phoenicians, but you don't hear about this. They want you to know about King Tut—and it's good to know about these civilizations, it's good to know about people all over the world, but first learn about *you*."

EMJ: *It's such a new experience for many students who are used to reading British or mainstream American literature. All of a sudden they see something written by a Chicano or a Chicana and they say, "That's me! And it's in writing."*
DM: That's right. I wanted to get Mario Salas, city councilman in San Antonio and a former Black Panther, to speak to my class because he wrote a sequel to Mary Shelley's *Frankenstein,* based on the philosophy of human values and the inner conflicts. He says that it's totally geared towards young readers, and he's looking for sponsors because he wants to publish the sequel. I thought that was very interesting. I have not read it; it's not published yet, but I said I need to go talk to that guy. I wonder where he's coming from, writing a sequel to Mary Shelley's *Frankenstein. Frankenstein* is one of the texts that I taught and related to current issues, to issues of self-identity and all the human needs that make up what we call "human." Humans are more than just the body. They need love and they need warmth and they need touch. We talk all about that and students latch on to it.

You can relate to British literature. Once they cut through the language and start understanding what's going on, they love Chaucer because you're teaching them sex, vulgarity, infidelity, irreverence—all the things that make up teenage rebellion. They're like, "This is classical literature?" Once you sell them on that, boy, you can sell them on a lot of things. I read them Robert Graves, World War I poetry, and two of my students got hooked on war poets from the various wars.

EMJ: *What advice would you give to aspiring writers, students who want to start writing?*
DM: Just do it. It took me a long time to get to the point where I didn't care. Because writers are like other people, we're always looking for approval and acceptance and people saying, "Yeah, you hit that right on the head as far as I'm concerned." It took me a long time to not care what other people had to say because there will always be critics whose job it is to say, "Well, this could be better." That's their life.

I would say, "Just write." I do think that sharing with a group is important, but ultimately you are in control of what you create. So then it becomes a matter of deciding, "Do I keep it this way?" Maybe if you're open-minded to suggestions, you may change it, but ultimately you are in control. The important thing is to realize that your life experiences have value for someone out there, and that there is someone out there who is having the same experience as you. All the good writing that I've seen, the classics, they all have some kind of tension, some conflict, some human turmoil, and that's not any different from what Latinos and Chicanos experience because we're ultimately very, very human. The way that we express it may be different, but the experience essentially is a human experience.

Part of my talk yesterday was about codes, internal codes. This goes back to reading *The Autobiography of Malcolm X*, which says that we have to recognize the internalized mechanisms that make us tick, that make us speak and act in this fashion or in that fashion. We have to recognize these internalized mechanisms because some of them keep us down. They keep us oppressed, and in oppressing oneself, one, in turn, oppresses an entire society. By the same token, if you're told constantly that your Spanish is not the correct Spanish, and you internalize that mechanism, in the end you're the one who's going to lose out. Those are some of the things I wanted to say yesterday about the codes, codes that say, "You can't write about that, and you can't express this in this way, and what is your mother going to think?" and, "What's wrong with you?" because that was one of the questions that was constantly asked of me.

NS: *Gloria Anzaldúa, in* Borderlands, *talks a lot about language. "So if you want to really hurt me, talk badly about my language. Ethnic identity is twin skin to linguistic identity—I am my language."[3] You also have said that when your use of Spanish is criticized, you and your identity are being criticized as well.*

DM: Right. I tell my students language is a living, breathing thing; it changes. We change, language changes. I can go back and think of words that we used when we were growing up that are no longer in use or now they have different connotations. One time in El Paso, I thought I was being insulted in Spanish when someone came and said to me "mochate." I said, "What?" "Mochate." I was ready to go, "Blah, blah, to you too!" when all the person was saying was "share." It was the slang word for "share" or "Are you going to treat me?" Over here we would say "tritriar," "treat, let's go treat." I was looking at this man because I thought he had insulted me.

But yes, I agree with Gloria and say that if you insult my language, if you insult the way I express myself, then you're insulting who I am. It took me a long time to start braiding the language, but I'm also proud of the fact that I can go back and speak Elizabethan and go through the Baroque Spanish. I admire Sor Juana Inés de la Cruz's life story—her writing was just way before her time. I wish she lived now. I admire her greatly.

NS: *I've noticed you've used the terms Chicano, Latino, and Hispanic. What is the label that you prefer?*
DM: I'm Chicana. I'm also aware of the fact that there are a lot of young people that just don't know where the word came from. My grandfather was using the word "chicano/chicana" when we were young. He gave me one of my first lessons in linguistics when he said that the Native American Indians in Mexico had no "X" in pronunciation and they had no "J." When the Spanish came along, they were going "mechica, mechicano, soy mechicano," rather than "soy Azteca." When people were migrating over here, they dropped the "me" and it became "chicano/chicana." He said that back in the early 1900s it was very popular to say "chicano/chicana"—it was a very proud term. Somewhere along the way people came out and said that it is derogatory, that its meaning comes from the word pig, and I'm like, "No, no, my grandfather wouldn't call us pigs"!

I also started doing some research of the terms that were applied to Latinos and Mexican Americans according to the census. At one point we were Latins, then we were Latin Americans. In the following census, we became "white," but "of Latin origin," and then they subcategorized the word: Mexican, Dominican, Cuban, Puerto Rican, or Other. Then the term Hispanic came around. It originated with the United States Census Bureau, which sent out a sample, I believe it was under Reagan, to seven hundred households in the Florida area and seven hundred more in the New Mexican area. They gave people a list of terms that they identified with, and Hispanic came up on top.

Hispanic is an umbrella, catchall phrase. I personally don't like it, but I use it because that's what my students use. Personally, if I can't use Chicana, I'd rather be called Latina, and not Mexican American either. Mexicans are Americans. You know, "somos de las Américas." So it's redundant to me. I'm not a hyphenated American. I am a fifth-generation Tejana; I'm very proud of it. Go tell me what's American anymore? I tell that to my students, "You know, you need to learn your history." I'm just getting them to think on their own. I took them to the section in the library where they can research their genealogy, including the Native American, and trace it as far back as we can go. I firmly believe that that's the key, or one of the keys. They need to know the other part of their history, not just the Hispanic part. Listen, "His-panic," you do linguistics.

NS: *Her-spanic.*
DM: Yeah, her-spanic, his-panic, I'm no one's panic.

SELECTED WORKS BY DIANA MONTEJANO

Poems
"Chencha of the Earth Diana." *Blue Mesa Review* 9 (1998).
"La Fiebre." *Blue Mesa Review* 9 (1998).
Nebulous Thoughts. Albuquerque, NM: Mano Izquierda Books, 1987.
"Una oración en la tempestad." In *Cantos al sexto sol: A Collection of Aztlanahuac Writings,*
    edited by Cecilio Garcia Xilo Camarillo, Roberto Rodríguez, and Patrisia Gonzales,
    201. San Antonio, TX: Wings Press, 2002.

NOTES

1. "Making Connections and Reconnections: Reasons Why I Write" (talk presented at
    Texas A&M University–Corpus Christi, September 30, 1999).
2. Ibid.
3. Gloria Anzaldúa, *Borderlands/La Frontera: The New Mestiza* (San Francisco: Spinsters/
    Aunt Lute Books, 1987), 59.

Pat Mora, © Cheron Bayna

"YOU MUST BE THE CHANGE YOU WISH TO SEE IN THE WORLD"

Conversation with Pat Mora

Pat Mora's work is undeniably rooted in the desert, the people, and the stories of the Southwest. This setting provides the perfect arena for her to explore the personal and social ramifications of bilingualism and biculturalism. Placing Mexican and European American cultures into a dialogue, Mora seeks to build bridges, initiate conversations, and foster communication. In her collection of essays, Nepantla *(1993), she explains that the poet is a modern-day curandera, or spiritual healer, and the book contains one of the most provocative descriptions of the writer's task. Mora writes, "The Chicana writer seeks to heal cultural wounds of historical neglect by providing opportunities to remember the past, to share and ease bitterness, to describe what has been viewed as unworthy of description, to cure by incantations and rhythms, by listening with her entire being and responding. She then gathers the tales and myths, weaves them together, and, if lucky, casts spells."*

Mora's writing has won many critical awards and prestigious fellowships. Her latest collection, Adobe Odes, *won the 2007 International Latino Book Award for Best Poetry in English. Additionally she won the 2006 National Hispanic Cultural Center Literary Award, a National Endowment for the Arts (NEA) Creative Writing Fellowship, and the Premio Aztlán Literature Award. Mora is the recipient of a*

Kellogg National Leadership Fellowship to study ways of preserving cultures. She is also a prolific writer of over thirty children's books, including The Night the Moon Fell *(2000), a picture book that retells the Mopan Maya myth of the creation of the Milky Way, and, most recently,* Let's Eat! A Comer! *(2008), the first in a new series of bilingual books for young children,* My Family*Mi Familia. *She authored a memoir,* House of Houses *(2001), which chronicles her experiences of growing up on the Texas-Mexico border. She is a native of El Paso, Texas, and received her BA and an MA in English from the University of Texas at El Paso, where she was an administrator and director of the Centennial Museum. As a consultant to the W. K. Kellogg Foundation, she worked on U.S.-Mexico youth exchanges. Mora has taught English at all levels and has held a Distinguished Visiting Professorship at the University of New Mexico. Her commitment to work with and for children as well as to promote literacy manifests itself in her founding of El día de los niños/El día de los libros, now housed with the American Library Association. She lives in the Northern Kentucky area and Santa Fe, New Mexico.*

In this interview, which we conducted when she visited the campus of Texas A&M University–Corpus Christi in March of 2000, Mora discusses her ongoing concern with literacy and her work with educators, reflecting further on the large-scale implications of the lack of Mexican Americans in the publishing industry. She also comments on her writing in different genres and her choice of Spanish and English as determined by considerations of her audience. Primarily writing for English-dominant readers, she nonetheless frequently uses bilingual play to create humor. Growing up on the border and in the desert, she claims, has led to her preoccupations with internal and external spaces, now a staple of her poetry. Finally, Mora addresses her interest in Eastern philosophy and her attempts to transcend conflict and construct wholeness.

NS: *Why did you become a writer, or when did you become aware that you could write?*

PM: I've always joked that I became a writer when I saw the age of forty coming at me. There's a lot of truth to that. I had thought about writing, I would say, when I graduated from eighth grade. My parents gave me a typewriter, and they gave me this very pretty stationery. I clearly remember that they had a party for me, and after people left, I sat there and wrote all of this rhyming, religious poetry, which, when I thought back on it after writing *Aunt Carmen's Book of Practical Saints*, was an interesting circle.

I am not a good journal keeper unless I'm out of the country, but I would write myself notes when my children were little, and it's been of interest to me that the few scraps I kept are related to the genres that I write in. I would say, "This would make a good poem," or "This would make a good essay," or "This would make a good children's book." So the interest was there. The love of language is really the main reason that I am a writer. I love reading; it's one of the great forces that has shaped me. At a certain point I thought, "Gosh, my life is soon going to be half over, and I want writing to be part of it."

I used to love to cook—I still do, but I don't cook as often. So I put on the outside of the kitchen cabinet this quote from Cervantes, "By the Street of By and By you arrive at the House of Never," as a way to put pressure on myself so that I couldn't just keep saying, "Well, one day I'll do it." I began by taking tiny bits of time, by saying, "I will spend an hour on the weekend." It was also at a time in my life when I was going through a divorce. I think those two things came together.

EMJ: *You've written many collections of poetry, but also a memoir and a collection of essays,* Nepantla.
PM: With the essays I thought about whether they could be useful. Many of them were based on speeches, and I had just thought, "Well, could they be useful if they were written down, either for people working with Latino students or people interested in youth?" The *use* is very important for me. The memoir was a total surprise. It was not a book I ever expected to write. I've said that perhaps the death of my father was the impetus. I had really started doing some tape recording before he died, and I had received an NEA. I had gone to Santa Fe, I had a little time off, and I was living in this wonderful, charmed place, a wonderful adobe with a wonderful garden. It was the perfect place for me to work on this book. But indeed when I work in prose—I'm going to try other books in prose—I always feel that it's a bit like being in cobwebs. I'm always saying to myself, "But don't worry because when you finish this, you can go back to poetry."

I love the white space on the page. I love feeling that I can shape that space in all kinds of ways. Maybe that has to do with the whole interest in space and geography and coming from the desert. I love that expansiveness.

EMJ: *Is the writing process different for you whether you write poetry or prose?*

PM: I consider poetry the ultimate challenge because you're trying to do so much with fewer words. I love the challenge of it. And I think that writing poetry improves all writing. I always say that to students. It makes you so conscious of the weight of every word and the sound of every word.

But there are some things that don't lend themselves to poetry as much. I guess the memoir could have been written as poetry, but that would have limited its audience in a way. So in that sort of organic sense, it's trying to find which genre is going to be most appropriate for the notion that you've begun to play with.

NS: *Have you ever started a poem and then turned it into prose or a narrative?*

PM: Not really, probably because I'm very goal-oriented. I don't tend to give myself the luxury of, "Oh, well, just write experimentally." I'm usually focused on working toward a book. Right now, for example, I'm hoping that my next book of poems for adults will be a book of odes, à la Neruda's *Elemental Odes*. It's a nice time in my life to think about what are all the things I love. So most of my writing then gets shaped by the project ahead. I think it has to do with the sense of urgency that I have about this kind of work.

EMJ: *What other prose pieces are you attempting?*

PM: This is risky to even talk about. But I have mentioned in the course of being here that I do a lot of work with teachers and librarians. I'm very interested in them because, of course, they are preparing our next generation, not only of college students, but of readers. I listen to educators. I always learn from them, and indeed it was a librarian in Ohio who one day said to me, "Why is it that you write poetry for adults and not for children?" I had never thought about it. I had been writing for children, but not poetry for children. So that really led me to write *Confetti*.

A couple of years ago a librarian in California said to me, "There is so little out about Latina teenagers. Why don't you think about writing something?" That stayed with me. I am playing with doing a novella, in a diary format, which no editor may want to publish. I'm very interested in the internal voice and how I might create a character so that we can hear her on the inside. I don't tend to be plot driven. When people say to me, "Well, what's gonna happen?" I have to admit that plots really are not of huge interest to me. Now, unfortunately, that may be a problem. We are so plot driven because of movies and speed and all of this, but that doesn't interest me as much. I have been playing with a book about a thirteen-year-old girl. I feel I know her pretty well; she's a real sweetheart, an introvert by nature, and I am just trying to let us hear her. This would interest me.

NS: *You write mostly in English, but at times you switch to Spanish. How would you describe your use of the two languages?*
PM: I'm writing to a great extent for an English-speaking audience. I am bilingual, though English dominant. I'm interested in including Spanish because it's part of my world, it's part of my mind. On the other hand, I am not writing for a primarily Spanish-speaking audience, or I would be writing in Spanish. To use *House of Houses*, I built in humor for the person who is bilingual. There is subversion in the use of Spanish, very consciously.

NS: *Do you go back and look at your writing again and think, "This is going to work better with a Spanish word"?*
PM: Sometimes. And sometimes an editor might mention it. For example, my editor at Beacon does not read Spanish, but she gives me free rein. Her assistant editor at the time was African American, so that was interesting. My editor would read it, then her assistant editor would read it, and sometimes the assistant editor would say, "I can't follow along enough. I need a little more help." So then I might go in and add a word or look at context clues to make sure that, yes, there was going to be double pleasure if you were bilingual, there were going to be times in which you were going to get to savor things in a special way, but that on the other hand if you weren't bilingual, you could stay with me because I want that.

Particularly after I left Texas and moved to the Midwest, I was aware of people who were very interested in the Latina experience but had never even heard Spanish around them, whereas in Texas we would say, "Well, people have heard it," and they could piece things together. But I think in the Midwest I became aware of many people who were very interested, but they wanted to be able to follow along.

Also, the characters influence the language. If the character is primarily Spanish-speaking, I will use more Spanish because I hear her or him that way. In New Mexico you often have someone who is second or third generation—there they would say hispanos—who may spend most of their lives in English. That was sort of a surprise to me but influenced the language in *Aunt Carmen's Book of Practical Saints.* The speaker is a fictional character, but I used that as a guide in creating her.

NS: *Several of your poems in* Borders, *two in particular, are very intimate, one about divorce and one about cancer. There was no Spanish at all in either. I was wondering if the topic determines or influences which language is used.*

PM: Only a good critic is going to be able to go back and tell me some of those things that I not only don't notice but don't want to notice. But if the question were, "Do I think that the level of intimacy affects the use of Spanish?" my initial reaction would be, "No," because I have written some very intimate poems, particularly about relatives, that do have a lot of Spanish. In fact the tribute to my father in *Agua Santa* is the only poem—a long poem—I have attempted that is totally in Spanish. I did that on purpose because I wanted to do something special in his memory. It was a very tough thing for me to do, a totally new form. I don't think the issue is intimacy, but it might have to do with the nature of the topic.

EMJ: *Much of your writing seems to explore the concept of borders and border-lands—borders between people, between men and women, between the upper and the lower classes, between Mexican Americans and European Americans. Why is this concept of borders so important to you?*

PM: Because I am a border woman. I grew up moving back and forth between these two countries with ease. I always lived in the United States, but when you live on the border, you go to Mexico. It's very hard for people in the middle of the United States to understand. I say in *Nepantla* that I was blessed that I could look at the country of my grandparents all the time, which many Americans cannot do. On the campus at which I went to school and where I worked, you actually look out at these very poor colonias on the other side of the Rio Grande. I've always had that sense that I could have been born on the other side. So borders interest me.

EMJ: *That ties in with the issue of space you mentioned earlier, your interest in space and geography. It's not just the landscapes of the Southwest, especially the desert and its fauna that keep recurring in your poetry, but also the private spaces of the home. Your poetry contains many spatial metaphors, such as being*

on the edge, being in between, on living "in a doorway," as you say in your poem
"Sonrisas." How does space figure in your writing?

PM: Consciously I wasn't that aware of the interest except when I began to realize, again when I left the desert, how I would feel every time I returned. Every time I saw that plane begin to land and I would look out at this tremendous space and think how totally I felt at home there. Many of my Midwestern friends would confide to me that they found the desert sometimes even terrifying. I remember one of the brightest women I know, an academic in Cincinnati, who said to me that the first time she came to the Southwest she was afraid she would fall off because she was so used to the protection of trees. I do say in *House* that I think geography shapes us; our early geography shapes us in complex ways.

When I taught at the University of New Mexico this past fall, I had the pleasure of creating a course on a topic of my choice, and the course I created was called "Spirit and Space," in preparation for another book. I do want to do another book of prose, one that portrays the desert as a place of contemplation. I want to look at the whole tradition of the desert fathers or of Christ going into the desert, and the tradition of the desert as a negative space—the desert of my life, the desert of a relationship—that creates this parched sense. I want to flip that a bit and play with what the gifts are that the desert offers.

You're right, I'm very interested in internal space, intensely interested in that. I'm very interested in one's internal rooms, issues of the psyche. I'm a big fan of *The Poetics of Space* by Bachelard. It's very important to me—the world of dreams, mental space. I think it comes from being a reader. True readers have that introspective interest in space, the space of the page.

EMJ: *Space has also become more politicized and can be viewed in a geopolitical sense, especially of course the space of the border. In your poem "Sonrisas," for example, you describe the speaker as positioned between two very different rooms. Is there a political message?*

PM: Well, the idea of claiming space is a big issue, certainly a big issue for Chicanas. There's a lot of discomfort sometimes, and I encounter that even with highly successful professionals who are reluctant to claim space, who see it as inappropriate, who will say things like, "Well, we've been taught not to do that." But I'm also interested in how we really claim our internal space, and that can have everything to do with reproductive questions, but it also works psychologically. It's very complex because of patriarchy.

NS: *Gloria Anzaldúa speaks about the conflict a border person experiences and the "linguistic terrorism" associated with it. She portrays a constant conflict within herself on the issue of identity, belonging. The dual identity of a border person leads her to note, ". . . sometimes I feel like one cancels out the other and we are zero, nothing, no one."*[2]
PM: Or the flip, "I belong in both." It's in *Nepantla* that I say, "On a good day, it's double pleasure in a way. I have the advantage of moving back and forth." Then there are situations where, yes, it's plenty difficult. I don't know at this point in my life whether I would say "in conflict." I don't know that I would use that language. I would say that there are "conflicts" involved for all of us, and how we negotiate space. That's really what we're talking about. There are conflicts.

NS: *Do you feel the psychological turmoil Anzaldúa writes about with respect to ethnic and cultural identity?*
PM: I think it has to do with time in life. At this time I'm really interested in how we construct wholeness. I've become very interested in Zen and that whole idea of how we honor the self and how we reflect on the self. In a way it's an issue that incorporates ethnicity or gender or class, but it also includes the challenge of being human.

NS: *Anzaldúa also writes a great deal on language issues.*
PM: These have all been issues for me. I wouldn't ever want to seem Pollyannish about it. These are intense issues for me, obviously, whether I'm talking about writing for children or writing for adults. I deal with them all the time, almost on a daily basis. I'm interested in the political issues. But within the last couple of years I've become very interested also in some philosophical issues. They are related, but they are different approaches to the same thing.

One of the most important quotes in my life for the last two or three years has been from Gandhi, "You must be the change you wish to see in the world." I'm very interested in exploring that. But given what I have experienced, given what I have inherited, given the privilege I've had, given the scars I may carry, what is it that I can best do? What is the change that I wish to explore?

NS: *Do Mexican American writers face different problems from those of main-stream writers in getting published?*

PM: Definitely. Oh, definitely. In spite of all these comments about the "Latin Boom," or whatever, all you have to do is look at the numbers. For example, the Academy of American Poets does not have a single Latino on its letterhead—not a chancellor, not a member of their honorary board. Why? Because, they would tell you, there isn't one who is good enough. They might not say it publicly, but believe me, they would say it privately. They would think, "If there were one good enough, we'd have them." We're talking about what is probably the most prestigious of the poetry organizations that affect fellowships, awards, everything.

In this state [Texas], the most important children's book award is the Bluebonnet Award, which began in 1979. In the history of that award, I believe one Mexican American has been on the committee that picks the twenty books that the children will vote on. Nobody seems to notice that! I'm always sitting there thinking, "How can this be?" I always feel, "Why is it that people aren't ashamed?" That's my response. And there are a lot of publications that I almost don't let myself look at now because I would get so upset. Instead, I say to myself, "Well, take that same money and give it to National Council of La Raza. Why take that publication if it's just going to drive you crazy?"

So it does remain very, very hard, and in part I have become more and more convinced that until Latinos are part of the entire publishing indus-try, I don't know how much change will take place. That is, until they are bookstore owners, manage Barnes and Noble, become the vice-president of Borders, until that happens. Between now and then, I spend a lot of time talking about the kinds of actions that people can take. People can go to the manager of their local bookstore and say, "Why is it we have all these col-umns of books on African Americans, gays/lesbians, and Native Americans, and yet look at the population here!"

NS: *Teachers can go to their school boards and say, "We need more literature that interests us."*

PM: You bet they can! And they can talk to these publishers that wine and dine them, look them right in the eye and ask, "How diverse is your editorial staff?" I say to them, "Ask impertinent questions." That's a tough request. But I get these catalogues from major publishing companies that list the books for fall, the books for spring, and there will be one book by a Latino. And we know what the demographics of this country are. We have a long way to go.

NS: *As a linguist, I'm interested in labels, "Chicana," "Mexican American," "Latina." My students often have trouble with the terminology. What term do you feel is most appropriate?*

PM: I'm very comfortable if people say "Chicana, Latina, Mexican American." I don't have any trouble with those. "Hispanic" I have more problems with. In the introduction to *Nepantla*, I talk a little bit about that. I don't resent it. For example, publishers like the word "Hispanic." There are certain campuses that like the word "Hispanic." The problem with the word is that when we celebrated the Quincentenary in 1992, there was a big discussion because the word connotes European. It connotes, whether we want it to or not, middle class; it connotes pride in European roots, which means, "I am connected to Spain," when in truth most of us are that grand mestizaje, la mezcla, a mix. To be more proud of the Spanish side than of the indigenous side bothers me a lot. "Latina" is a word that right now seems to be more encompassing, but five years from now it may be another word, and I'm very comfortable with that. I think language is fluid, but I also believe that people have a right to their own self-referents. I'm not the kind that scolds students, and I know there are people who do and say, "You should say Chicana." I feel people need to come to their own decision about their identity, but part of our responsibility as academics is to help them see the connotation of these words. People are choosing the words for particular reasons, and students need to be aware of those fine distinctions.

SELECTED WORKS BY PAT MORA

Poetry
Adobe Odes. Tucson: University of Arizona Press, 2006.
Agua Santa: Holy Water. Boston: Beacon Press, 1995. Rpt. Tucson: University of Arizona Press, 2007.
Aunt Carmen's Book of Practical Saints. Boston: Beacon Press, 1997.
Borders. Houston: Arte Público Press, 1993.
Chants. Houston: Arte Público Press, 1984.
Communion. Houston: Arte Público Press, 1991.

My Own True Name: New and Selected Poems for Young Adults. Houston: Arte Público Press, 2000.

Memoir
House of Houses. Boston: Beacon Press, 2001.

Children's Books
El árbol de Pablo. New York: Scholastic, 1996.
The Bakery Lady. Houston: Piñata Books, 2001.
A Birthday Basket for Tía. Orlando: Harcourt, 1999.
Confetti: Poems for Children. New York: Lee and Low Books, 1999.
The Desert Is My Mother: El desierto es mi madre. Houston: Piñata Books, 1994.
Let's Eat! ¡A Comer! New York: Rayo Books, 2008.
A Library for Juana: The World of Sor Juana Inés. New York: Alfred Knopf, 2002.
Listen to the Desert: Oye al desierto. New York: Clarion Books, 1994.
¡Marimba! Animales From A–Z. New York: Clarion Books, 2006.
Maria Paints the Hills. Santa Fe: Museum of New Mexico Press, 2002.
The Night the Moon Fell. Toronto: Groundwood Books, 2000.
Pablo's Tree. New York: Simon and Schuster, 1996.
The Race of Toad and Deer. Toronto: Groundwood Books, 2001.
Tomás and the Library Lady. New York: Houghton Mifflin, 2001.
Uno, Dos, Tres: One, Two, Three. New York: Clarion Books, 2000.

Essays
Nepantla: Essays from the Land in the Middle. Albuquerque: University of New Mexico Press, 1993.

NOTES

1. *Nepantla: Essays from the Land in the Middle* (Albuquerque: University of New Mexico Press, 1993), 131.
2. Gloria Anzaldúa, *Borderlands/La Frontera*, 2nd ed. (San Francisco: Aunt Lute Books, 1999), 85.

Benjamin Sáenz, © Arturo Enriquez

BETWEEN BELONGING AND EXILE

Conversation with Benjamin Alire Sáenz

Benjamin Alire Sáenz is a poet, short story writer, essayist, novelist, and author of children's books. His work evokes the landscape of the southwestern United States, the desert, the cities (El Paso, Juárez), and the mountains. This border area between the United States and Mexico, a place that harbors extremes of poverty, violence, and crime, serves as the setting for his characters' search for community and their struggles to find identity and self-worth in a society that continuously places that self-worth into doubt. In both his poetry and his fiction, Sáenz celebrates the accomplishments of the ordinary people that populate this place.

Sáenz grew up in the desert in southern New Mexico. He received a BA from St. Thomas Seminary in Denver, Colorado, and continued his studies at the University of Louvain in Belgium. He holds an MA from the University of Texas at El Paso, studied American Literature at the University of Iowa, and was awarded a Wallace E. Stegner Fellowship in Poetry at Stanford University, before returning to El Paso to teach creative writing. He has published four collections of poetry, including Calendar of Dust *(1991), which won the Americas Book Award in 1992. His most recent collection is entitled* Dreaming the End of War *(2006). He has also authored four critically acclaimed novels, among them* Sammy and

Juliana in Hollywood *(2006). The book was a finalist for the Los Angeles Times Book Award and was also named one of the top ten books of the year by the American Library Association. Sáenz published a book of short stories,* Flowers for the Broken *(1992), and has two bilingual children's books,* A Gift from Papa Diego *(1998) and* Grandma Fina and Her Wonderful Umbrellas *(2001). The latter was named the best children's book of 1999 by the Texas Institute of Letters.*

Much of this interview, which took place on the campus of Texas A&M University–Corpus Christi in March of 2007, revolves around Sáenz's reflections on language and various forms of nationalism. His poetic practice is predicated on his view of language as a living, constantly shifting phenomenon. He explains how his community first taught him to appreciate the spoken word and to embrace multilinguality, concerns that he now seeks to share with his students. Countering nationalist attitudes toward language, Sáenz places languages and language attitudes in an international context. He further discusses the representational value the border holds in much contemporary theorizing and adamantly insists on its materiality, of which he is reminded daily.

EMJ: *I'm intrigued by something you wrote in your essay "Notes from the City in Which I Live," "This city on the border . . . has given me words. I return them to the city."¹ What do you mean by that?*
BAS: I think one of my fascinations with words and language came from the fact that I was bilingual. When you are a kid you think your reality is universal, and then you find out, no, it's not, it is just specific to my little community. It's not universal at all. I remember when I first met someone that was Jewish. I thought everybody was Catholic.

When coming to language, I realized for instance that I resisted Spanish in some ways. But I liked Spanish in other ways. I adored my grandparents—they only spoke Spanish. So it was their language, and I respected and loved that—that's how I communicated with someone I loved. At home, my parents spoke both languages. My father in particular was a huge code switcher, huge. He would say things as I was growing up like, "Está ringando telefón." The correct use is, "Está sonando el teléfono." He didn't even say "teléfono," he said "telefón"; my mother says "telefón," which is right in between two worlds. I got a big kick out of that.

I have friends, other Chicanos I grew up with, who liked to play with language. I remember very specifically that one friend liked the play of words between Spanish and English. He'd sing the song, "Quantanamera, yo soy un hombre sincero," and he would say, "I am a man without zero." I loved his humor! There's a little restaurant called the Nopalito, and he would call it the "No Little Stick." I thought this guy was a little genius. I loved his jokes and I was really attracted to the wordplay, the interconnections between languages. I was drawn to the way people spoke, for instance cuss words in English and in Spanish. I was very analytical. I wouldn't just say, "This is the F-word"; I would turn it around and wonder, "Where did that come from? What is that?" I would study it, the phonetic thing about it, in my mind. It was very interesting to me.

I love the way people spoke, and I love the sayings, so I listened and remembered them. My grandmother spoke in sayings; she would say, "¿Como va el dicho?" and she would come out with her little saying about something or another, and my mother did too. My mother and my father spoke differently. My mother's family is from an old traditional Hispanic family of New Mexico farmers. Some of her words are not so much pochismos, as we would say; they're old Spanish. Like the past tense of "traje" in Old Spanish is "truje." That's not slang; it's archaic Spanish. She uses some of that when she speaks. There are also the oral traditions, the stories they used to tell us, which I liked. They used to scare me. They were designed to scare us, frankly, into behaving. You know, they used those stories of la llorona and the story about the devil in Texas—all of those things to scare us. Whatever their original intention in the oral tradition was, they were manipulated to get us to behave. I did not understand that until later, but I was fascinated with the stories.

NS: *Did they work?*
BAS: No. Absolutely not [laughs], but I gave them all an A for effort. So I believe that when I came to writing eventually, I understood languages fully. My experiences in Europe helped, trying to struggle with French, which I never really conquered, or learning some Dutch that's practical. When you learn how to say a new word in that language as an adult, language becomes so visible, and you say, "Wow, that's a great way to say that," because we don't say it that way, and you realize that language is untranslatable. Language is not just an accidental way of saying something in this way; it's a worldview, it's an entire worldview. The fact that the moon in Italian and French and Spanish is gendered is a worldview, and that it isn't in English is a worldview. You can have equivalents sometimes, but you cannot translate.

So I came to this understanding of language and my knowledge of languages because of the communities I lived in and their code switching. They gave me a love of language; they made language visible to me. And I understand that words don't originate with me; they are passed down to me and I use them and that means I belong. Language, whether we like it or not, or know it or not, is really important. Richard Rodríguez said something in his first book that I most vehemently disagreed with—that Spanish is a private discourse. What made him a public man is the English discourse. So I asked, "Richard, since when is Spanish not a public discourse? What are you talking about? You are not being very smart about the way you analyze any language because it is all public discourse, and ideas of private and public are constructed by a community that's public."

EMJ: *That seems to go along with language policies in the southwestern United States and in this country in general.*
BAS: It does. But these are issues of racism, which is what he wants to erase. He doesn't want to go there. So he wants to frame it in terms of these "nonpolitical" ways. But it's just not accurate.

NS: *Did education strip you of this other language? Diana Montejano, a poet from San Antonio, said that she was punished for speaking Spanish.*
BAS: She is my student. I directed her thesis. I love her work.

NS: *She said that in addition to physical punishment, in high school the students were fined when they spoke Spanish.*
BAS: We weren't; it wasn't that bad. It was more subtle, though when I went to school it was pretty much segregated. I went to a small school, and there was more or less a gringo first grade and a Mexican first grade. They would track you. Sometimes they would put a gringo in with the Mexicans and a Mexican in with the gringos; they would switch us, but they were still tracking. I started there in 1960, and there were subtle signs—we knew not to speak Spanish. It simply was understood. We didn't talk about things like racism, but it was there. I always considered our teachers, many of whom were transplants, like missionaries, and I think they considered themselves to be missionaries as well.

It became less and less true as we moved up, though I think that our teachers had very low expectations of us. This is one of the reasons I wrote

Sammy and Juliana in Hollywood. It is true to my educational experiences in terms of the teachers, some of whom had racist attitudes, and some of them just hated us. I don't think they just hated us because we were Mexicans; I think that's way too simplistic. It was also the sixties, and they hated popular culture. They hated the fact that students have a culture, and it's not just dominant culture, it's popular culture, and they hated our popular culture. They hated the way we dressed. They hated our music. To us that meant they hated us. So they should not have been surprised that we hated them back—we were kids! The whole educational system did not encourage us to be bilingual. That is certainly true. But I took Spanish all the way through school. I read stories and literature in Spanish all through high school because I was in Spanish 4 and Spanish 5. I was tracked there too. There was Spanish 1, Spanish 2, and then it was S or E for dominant Spanish speakers or dominant English speakers. But that was fine; I think that makes sense. I don't think that is discrimination. It has to do with whether you already speak Spanish, then you're at a different level.

NS: *Many of my students in Corpus Christi who are in their late teens and early twenties don't speak Spanish, even though Spanish is their parents' first language. Their parents thought Spanish would hold them back, so when they were children, their parents didn't teach them Spanish, they only spoke English. I have a student who can't speak to her grandparents, but her mother now is insisting that her granddaughter—my student's daughter—learn Spanish. She's wondering, "What about me? Why didn't you teach me Spanish? You want your granddaughter to learn Spanish." And her mother says, "At the time we didn't want to hold you back."*

BAS: Well that's very true. People respond to discrimination in different ways. They may be inappropriate, but they don't want to be discriminated against. There is a lot of internalized racism in terms of language, as well as in terms of other things. When I was growing up, for instance, it was also skin color, the issue of mestizaje, the Indian issue. You don't want your child to be dark. People would say, "Qué bonito tu bebe, parese gringo." It means that your child is going to fit in. This is a direct response to the kind of racist attitude that people have toward darker skinned people.

EMJ: *In terms of languages, it seems that you are not only concerned with English and Spanish, or variations of Spanish. On your web site is a poem that goes, "I write in English, dream / in Spanish, listen to Latin chants." Later on in that piece you also refer to Swahili. What is it about words, about the different languages, that interests you?*

BAS: Yes, there *is* more than that; I do think that languages make us richer. We grow so defensive when we don't know a language. That is a big part of the English Only movement; it has such a defensive posture. "I only know one language. We should all just speak one language." That's ludicrous! That's ridiculous! There are many languages in the world, and we shouldn't extinguish them. Some languages are endangered species, and we should protect them. Just because I don't speak indigenous languages doesn't mean that I shouldn't value them. That's an attitude toward language. If you don't know a language, I tell my students, then at least listen to its sounds. My students will get defensive. They might say, "I didn't read this poem because it had a lot of Spanish words in it." I had one student who got mad because I wrote a poem—and it's ironic in that I am referring to neo-Nazism—and it ends, "Deutschland, Deutschland, über Alles." They said, "I don't know German," and I said, "I really don't either." So they said, "Well, you have these words, and it's frustrating," and I tell them, "In the age of information, look it up, or ask people." Their ungenerous attitude toward other languages is self-evident, and that's a problem. The problem isn't necessarily that they don't know other languages, the problem is that they're just so ungenerous. My response to people is, "Why are you so ungenerous when it comes to other ways of speaking and looking at the world?" They have no answer because I reframe the issue in ways that make them look bad, because I am not willing to concede moral high ground to that attitude. Because it is very small and mean, and I've lived with that meanness my whole life in the United States. I refuse it and I refute it.

EMJ: *So there is a didactic, a pedagogical angle to your work when you bring those issues into the foreground?*

BAS: It is good to do it through poetry, because it is very sneaky and artful. A poem has to be a poem and it has to be art, but a poem also has to say something. It has to do both.

EMJ: *When in your essay, "Notes From Another Country," you respond to one reader's reaction to the characters' sadness in your novel* In Perfect Light *by saying, "They live on the border!"[2] I thought of Gloria Anzaldúa's characterization of the border as "una herida abierta." Where does that sadness come from? And what are the origins of that violence? Are they the results of racism and discrimination?*

BAS: I think that people internalize the ways in which they are seen. I have always believed that there is an internalized racism. We internalize the way people look at us. Added to that is the fact that the border really is and has been a dumping ground for both countries. The people who have traditionally come to the United States and are still doing it, not legally, are the people that Mexico doesn't give a damn about. I don't make a distinction between economic and political refugees. Since when is economics apolitical? Since when? People who have come over traditionally are from the working classes, from the uneducated classes, and the border has a great concentration of generations of this. So you have basically a working class and very poor people, and the border becomes the dumping ground for both sides.

We don't figure into the politics of Texas. We're an afterthought. We're a huge population, and we are an afterthought. So the border becomes a difficult space that both countries are using as a dumping ground, as a safety valve if you will, and that creates poverty, real material poverty. It's been done for a long time. How do you recover from that? When the border has been a dumping ground, how can it be a place of investments? How do you turn that around? El Paso for the longest time was sold as a cheap labor town by its wealthy people, by its very leaders, and we are slowly turning that around. We no longer see that as a good thing, but to recover from that takes a long time. So there's this psychology born of that—that we have an inferiority complex, but that is not to say that the poverty and the pain and the violence that comes with the culture isn't real. It gets very complex. You see the river and what they do to the river—even the river is as poor as we are. You think, wow, how can this be a place where cultural capital is created? How can this be a rich, cultural place where literature is created and art is created? But, in fact, art and literature are amazing on the border, though that becomes invisible in so many ways.

I want people to see the border as a real place and not just as a metaphor. I really very much resent it when it is just a literary trope. I once asked a Catholic priest—I am Catholic—because I thought that the Catholic Church in general was supporting a right-wing agenda in the last election. I said, "Are the poor just a theological concept? Or are they real?" He didn't answer [laughs]. That's the problem with postmodernism, that everything just becomes a representative, an emblem of something. Is there really no such thing as literal reality? Sometimes good old Karl Marx and analyzing material reality sounds awfully good to me. But it sounds very retro—I know that Marx is dead, but maybe we should resurrect him or some of those ideas. So it's really important for me to live on the border because it feeds me, and I think that we all want to live in places that are important. As far as I am concerned, El Paso is the heart of Texas. It really is. No apologies to Austin.

EMJ: *Even if no structural changes are made to improve the situation of border residents, individual characters in your fiction do reach out across gender, ethnic, racial, and social differences. For instance, there are Jaime and Joann and the Central American immigrants in "Alligator Park"; David, the gringo lawyer, and Andrés, as well as Grace and Andrés, in* In Perfect Light—*they all begin to care for and start to learn from each other. There is also the alternate community at the end of the novel with Vincent and Liz who don't initially get along. Does the only hope lie in such individual acts of reaching out and healing?*

BAS: This book is very much my theology of grace. For me it is a very complicated thing—what is grace along the border? What is grace anywhere? What is the grace of God after all in a world where people like Mister are killed randomly? That killing was very deliberate, and it was very harsh. But it happens all the time. People could say, "Oh that is so coincidental," and you say, "Yeah . . . you are walking down the street, and you get shot—that happens." This kind of an accident is part of life. Why do we bracket that out as if it weren't part of life? We know people get killed every day in cruel and random ways. They didn't deserve it, and it has nothing to do with their virtue or lack thereof. You'd think that if anyone should meet a bad end in the novel it's Andrés—you'd think that he earned this. Then you realize that this is exactly when grace/Grace intervenes.

EMJ: *Don't they help each other though?*

BAS: Yes. It's a mutual thing. Grace doesn't want to live—she's so unsentimental that she doesn't realize how deeply loved she is. In some ways she is selfless. She doesn't sentimentalize her work and so doesn't realize how many people she's helped. She's one of those people who show up and just do their jobs. But that showing up and doing her job in an unemotional way is so helpful to people. When she loses her son, that's the first time she understands how valuable *her* life is. She has never understood her own life, never even understood how deeply in pain she was at losing her husband because she never really dealt with it. She was always Sam's widow; now she can be something more than Sam's widow. She can be alive, which is one of the ironies of the novel. It's about death, it's about life, it's about her attitude when she goes to Mass. She picked up the habit because Sam used to go, but Sam was sincere about it, whereas she just goes. And in her prayers she badgers God. She does! Her prayers are like, "Look, God, you better give me this; you are falling down on the job here." I really loved her character. One of the things I liked about writing her was that she wasn't a typical sentimental Mexican woman, because in literature I think that Mexican women are very sentimentalized. She's not just a mother; she's got a professional job. Even in women's literature we don't find women that are professionals. I don't know why that is. Grace is very, very practical, and we don't view Mexican women as very practical. But they are! I know many of them. They're not just women who call their sons "mi'jito" and "Come algo." "Eat, eat." She was a very important character for me to write.

NS: *I thought it was interesting how you bring in Grace's experiences at a university. When she did well, people would be surprised because she's a Mexican woman, surprised that she could be so successful. Did you experience this type of reaction?*

BAS: This was true for our generation. People were surprised at the success of many Mexican American students because they expected nothing of us. When I was in the seminary, *my* professors were surprised. There was writing across the curriculum—you study philosophy, art history, theology, and so on; you turn in essays on everything, and all of your tests are essays. My professors were surprised that I was so analytical. It took me a while to figure out why, and I finally thought, "Oh, because they didn't expect that from me." In terms of manipulating the English language, I was probably their best student. But they said, "Wow," and then they got over it. And that was fine, but I noticed that they were surprised.

EMJ: *There are several scenes in your work that take place on the international bridge that connects the U.S. and Mexico. Andrés, returning to El Paso, looks back at Juárez and forward to El Paso, and the narrator tells us that Andrés wonders if he would ever have a country. In the prologue to your collection of short stories, "Exile," you speak of Michael and the narrator on the bridge. What does the bridge represent to you?*

BAS: This is my favorite thing to do, and I do it in several books. The bridge connects something that is disconnected, but not naturally so. We want to bridge that disconnection, we say, but what is bridged is also unbridgeable in some ways. So long as we have a border, Juárez isn't just another city, it is in another nation. So long as the border exists, it is unbridgeable. We can cross, but we can only be visitors. So there it is: as long as we are in love with nationalisms and borders, then in fact we're saying, "Only some people can cross." I am always very clear about this: borders are for the poor. There are no borders for the rich. Whatever nation you live in, if you are wealthy the borders are not for you. We don't like to look at it that way, but it is absolutely true. I can go anywhere, and I am not even that wealthy, but I can go anywhere. Poor people don't enact laws, the ruling classes do. Borders don't affect the people who make laws; they are exempt. You can make any law when you are exempt.

EMJ: *In your poetry and your fiction, you also place the Texas/Mexico border into a broader context by including cross-cultural connections that introduce global and geopolitical reference points. For instance in the epilogue to your short story collection* Flowers of the Broken, *"Between Worlds," the main situation is a soccer game, where the players are from Central and South American nations, from, and I'm quoting your words, "another America," which you juxtapose to "this America." How do you see the relationship between "this America" and "that America?"*

BAS: It's so problematic, so ingrained in me that the United States is called "America," a term that we have absolutely misappropriated. We've colonized the word and don't think of Mexico as part of North America—we have always put Mexico separately. Rather than include Mexico in the concept of North America, we say "Latin America and Mexico," or "South America and Mexico." This is really interesting. How resentful so many Latin Americans are that the United States appropriates that term! I like to think of America in a more pan-American way, though that's not the way that we view it in the United States. I feel that the other America is invisible to so many Americans who don't even see it as another America. You see, if we call them Americans too, then they are our brothers and sisters, and then they really belong to us in ways that we want to linguistically keep them separate. We also linguistically distance people by calling them "illegal aliens." We can call them "undocumented workers," we used to say that in the eighties, but we've devolved. Now we've reverted back to "illegal aliens." It is this linguistic distancing, a linguistic dehumanizing that suggests that they do not belong to us, and when someone does not belong to us we can do anything we want to them because they are not our equal. It's very racist and very ungenerous.

NS: *Even the term* legal alien *is offensive. It seems to distance us, as if we were saying, "You're not quite one of us. We let you in legally, but you're not one of us."*

BAS: Right; to me that is bothersome. Part of what I do in my work is to try to make this connection visible because I believe strongly in that.

EMJ: *You've lived in Europe, in Denver, and in California. Has your life abroad and away from the border influenced your thinking about the place you returned to?*

BAS: I think so. There's that sense of belonging and also that sense of exile. I think that all of us live between belonging and exile, frankly. I think of myself in broader terms as I grow older, and, as an adult, I hope that we are not provincial. I find it problematic when people never move anywhere—although you can be quite cosmopolitan staying in one place; it depends on your mind and your attitude. For me, going to Denver, always knowing that the world was not about me was not a bad thing. When I came to the realization that I live in this piece of the world that's nowhere and to realize the world is over there—that was a good thing. Not everything is about you! The people who grow up in New York think that everything is about them—this is not a good thing [laughs]. The people in San Francisco too, they think there are only two kinds of people in the world: San Franciscans and those who want to be San Franciscans! This is problematic. Okay, so let's expand our horizons.

When I was in Denver, I realized that I was Catholic in very different ways than my colleagues, who were all very good decent Midwestern boys who had gone to Catholic schools. I never went to Catholic school because in my part of the world only wealthy people went to Catholic schools. In their part of the world, people just went to Catholic schools; it was part of the different culture. I was more of an underground Catholic, and my traditions were very different from theirs. So I had to learn about mainstream Catholicism, and I was always adjusting, which is not a bad thing. I never read the literature that had Mexican Americans in it, so I didn't think that literature was supposed to reflect me. This too was not a bad thing necessarily. The fact that things weren't about me has made me a certain kind of person.

I never considered myself an American. I was a Chicano, I was a Mexican American! Then I went to Europe, and I never felt so American! "Oh boy, am I American!" I said. It was really interesting. When I went to Tanzania for a summer, I never felt so western. They called us "Mzungus." There was no distinction between me and my friend Dick Bradley, a really great white boy from Oklahoma—we looked pretty much the same to them. We were both Mzungus, which means "European." We were white, we were not African. That's all there was to it. I thought from that perspective, "That's right, what is identity anyway?" I realized very quickly that it's not fixed, it's a shifting thing. It is always dialectical; it makes sense in a particular context and in relationship to your environment. Chicano identity in the environment of Tanzania means nothing.

It's the same with power relationships. I can't pretend that I am power-less in the classroom. That's ludicrous. But what does power mean? Well, it depends. You have a sphere of influence, and we should analyze that. How big is it? The more powerful, the bigger the sphere of influence. What kind of influence? The least powerful people have no sphere of influence and no mobility. The more powerful you are, the more mobile you are. The poor can't move. Take Katrina and look at the concept of mobility. That you can just leave is not a thought a lot of people entertain. It's so middle class. "Why didn't they just leave?" This question is a way for us to blame the victims. Well, let's think about why they didn't leave, let's analyze that.

NS: *"Elegy for Burciaga" is one of my favorite poems because it talks about border language and the English Only movement. You've mentioned that you write in English, but this poem has a lot of Spanish. Is this part of your challenge to students' attitudes regarding other languages? How concerned are you about whether your audience understands it or not?*
BAS: Well, sometimes I have to care because of my editors. I do Spanish in *Sammy and Juliana* more naturally. If it were up to me, I'd just do it and tell my editor to get over it: "You get it! Don't tell me just because of this you can't get the story." It's interesting because in *Sammy and Juliana,* which is

taught a lot, this is really big in the teachers' minds. Some of them have said, "So much Spanish." But there's not a lot of Spanish in that book, it's simply not true. There's some Spanish, and it's not italicized. I don't italicize if it's left up to me. If editors ask me why, I say, "Well, because you italicize a foreign language, and for the author Spanish is not a foreign language," and I just leave it at that. Sometimes I make compromises with my editors because I am not particularly difficult. I'll go, "Well, okay, I will concede this, let's move on." But left up to me, I always think that it's pretty well understood and I tend not to worry. I do have discussions with editors about these issues. Some of them leave me alone and some don't. To be fair to them, all of my editors love my work, and I am very grateful for that. They are real champions of my work. They don't want to put me in an ethnic niche; they think that I should be read by everyone.

I'm writing something new about a Chicano everyman. It's a dramatic monologue of Joe Chávez García and his family, and it is entitled "El Joe Chávez García Suffers From Increasing Bouts of Optimism." It's based on the way my father speaks, and he's always code switching.

NS: *You also use Spanish in* In Perfect Light. *Do you write in English first and then change some of the words into Spanish?*
BAS: No, it comes as I am writing. I never go back and put it in, never. That would ring false to me.

NS: *I liked how Spanish brought out emotions in characters in this book. You use it very rarely but with great effect. For example, when the doctor greets Grace with "Como estas?" she responds, "His Spanish comforted her even more than the ritual small talk."*[3]
BAS: It's a holy language for me. I think I use Spanish the way poets used to use Latin.

NS: *Diana Montejano said that the term code switching implies the use of slang. She refers to her use of English and Spanish as "braiding" and thinks this is a much more poetic way to look at it.*
BAS: And she braids it beautifully. I came to call it code switching when I entered academia. Some people call it caló, some call it Tex-Mex, some call it Spanglish. I don't like TexMex because I am Tejano now, though I was born

in New Mexico, and they have no corner on the market on that one. I don't think I called it anything. This was just the way people talked.

When I was at Stanford, we all had to take Old English, and if you learn anything in Old English, you learn that language evolves, it's not fixed. You can take the academy approach that the French use—as if it does them any good [laughs]! Anyway, in the Alsace-Lorraine region people mix French and German. Why? Well, it's obvious. Language is a fluid thing, and it belongs to everyone, and if you think you can legislate it, you've got another thing coming. That ideological view of language to me is small-minded and controlling and frustrating for them because they're on the losing end. There are so many different kinds of Spanish in the world today. Everyone uses it differently—the way the Cubans manipulate it, the way the Puerto Ricans manipulate it, the way Mexicans do, and even different parts within Mexico or Colombia. Are you going to say there is only one way to speak Spanish? There is one way to speak English? You can hold that view if you want to, but I don't know where it's going to get you. This whole mentality to me is very unfruitful and very uncreative. And yes, I do think that it's nice that you know the rules of the language. I do believe that we should learn those, but given that most people who live in these areas don't go to school at all, what are they going to do to them? Shoot them? Disapprove of them? Is this just another way of saying I'm better because I'm pure? And this in a post-national age where we are all infected with mestizaje. You want to talk about purity? That's crazy! None of us are pure anything. If you want to think, "I speak correct English" or "I don't mix the two," well, other people do it all the time. I have been on panels, and we go round and round, and I sometimes just sit there because I don't feel like going there today, and I think, "You can have your discussion." But look at what people do with language. The Chicanos, for example, they make up words, and you think, "Ha, ha, ha isn't that great? Isn't that creative?" People doing something with language means that language is alive.

NS: *Code switching does not necessarily mean that the person isn't fluent in either language.*
BAS: In many instances that does happen to be true, and this is the flipside—that there are many people along the border who know neither language really. They just don't. I like to tell my students, "You really need to

learn language, and you need to play with it, because if you don't conquer a language, language will beat the crap out of you your whole life." It's true, it will, and it does, and it continues to. I try to make words visible, just like your clothes. I had a student once who said, "Mr. Sáenz, you're smart," and I said, "How do you know I'm smart?" He said, "Because of the way you talk," and I said, "Yes, yes that's it. Now let's have a conversation, now you're getting it. You think I am smart because of the way I talk." I use words like "synechdoche" or "emblem" and explain these to them. We do the same thing when we teach. Students will express themselves well, and we think they are smart. In writing, though, there is some pretty vacuous correct English out there!

SELECTED WORKS BY BENJAMIN ALIRE SÁENZ

Novels
Carry Me Like Water. New York: HarperCollins Publishers, 2005.
The House of Forgetting. New York: HarperCollins Publishers, 1997.
Names on a Map. New York: Harper Perennial, 2008.
In Perfect Light. New York: Rayo/HarperCollins, 2005.

Short Stories
Flowers For the Broken. Seattle: Broken Moon Press, 1992.

Poetry
Calendar of Dust. Seattle: Broken Moon Press, 1991.
Dark and Perfect Angels. El Paso: Cinco Puntos Press, 1995.
Dreaming the End of War. Port Townsend: Copper Canyon Press, 2006.
Elegies in Blue. El Paso: Cinco Puntos Press, 2002.

Children's Books
A Gift From Papá Diego/Un regalo de papá Diego. El Paso: Cinco Puntos Press, 1998.
Grandma Fina and Her Wonderful Umbrellas/La abuela Fina y sus sombrillas maravillosas.
    El Paso: Cinco Puntos Press, 2001.
He Forgot To Say Goodbye. New York: Simon and Schuster, 2008.
Sammy and Juliana in Hollywood. New York: Rayo/HarperCollins, 2006.

Article
"In the Borderlands of Chicano Identity, There Are Only Fragments." In *Border Theory: The Limits of Cultural Politics,* edited by Scott Michaelsen and David E. Johnson, 68–96. Minneapolis: University of Minnesota Press, 1997.

NOTES

1. *Elegies in Blue* (El Paso: Cinco Puntos Press, 2002), 114.
2. See http://www.benjaminsaenz.com/Pages/BenHome.html.
3. *In Perfect Light* (New York: Rayo/HarperCollins, 2005), 72.

Sandra Cisneros, © Ray Santisteban

"MUY PAYASA"

Conversation with Sandra Cisneros

Sandra Cisneros is a nationally acclaimed poet, novelist, author of children's books, and short story writer who has greatly contributed to bringing the experiences of Mexican Americans in the urban barrios of Chicago and in the dusty towns of South Texas onto the national and the global stage. Her work is widely taught at all levels of the educational system and read in One City/One Book projects across the country. Cisneros specifically features the lives of women on the border: young girls pursuing artistic ambitions in an environment that doesn't much value intellectual work; border brides finding the courage to break away from abusive husbands; or girls painfully discovering their sexuality and women asserting theirs in a society that works to deny them such desires. By presenting such a multiplicity of voices, as well as models of femininity outside of wife- and motherhood, Cisneros simultaneously questions popular constructions of Mexican American womanhood.

Cisneros was born in Chicago and grew up as the only daughter in a family with seven children. Because of her Mexican-born father's restlessness, the family moved back and forth between Mexico City and Chicago. She received her BA in English from Loyola University of Chicago and an MFA in Creative Writing from the University of Iowa. She has worked as a teacher and counselor for high school dropouts, a college recruiter, arts administrator, and visiting author, teaching creative writing at all levels. She has published two collections of poetry, Loose Woman *(1994) and* My Wicked Wicked Ways *(1987), as well as a collection of short stories entitled* Woman Hollering Creek and Other Stories *(1991), which won numerous awards, including the PEN Center West Award for Best Fiction of 1991. She has also authored a children's book,* Hairs/Pelitos *(1994), and two novels,* The House on Mango Street *(1991), winner of the Before Columbus American Book Award, and* Caramelo *(2002), which was selected as notable book of the year by several national publications. Cisneros has held a prestigious MacArthur Foundation Fellowship and two National Endowment for the Arts fellowships for fiction and poetry. Her books have been translated into over a dozen languages. She lives in San Antonio, Texas, and is currently working on a collection of autobiographical essays, entitled* Writing in My Pajamas.

In this interview, conducted in San Antonio, Texas, in March of 2007, Cisneros conveys a strong sense of connection to a community of writers. This ethic of community manifests itself in her founding, in 1995, of the summer writers' workshop Macondo, recently featured in the publication Poets *and* Writers. *Macondo is designed for "writers working on geographic, cultural, societal and spiritual borders," and for those who share a "global sense of community."[1] She discusses the creation of her public persona, derived from her performances, and gives a glimpse of a vibrant cultural scene in San Antonio. She also talks about her use of language—English and Spanish—with an awareness of the global reader; her work delving into the complexities of Mexican history in* Caramelo; *as well as her preoccupation with space in her fiction following* The House on Mango Street.

NS: *It's nice that you give so much of your time to students and teachers. How do you keep up the energy with all of the interviews you do and everybody wanting a piece of you?*

SC: I sleep. I sleep more than most people do—I sleep a lot, and that's how I recharge. I also have a lot of animals, and animals are, you know, god. They're light. I have six dogs, four cats, and a parrot. So I just play. I used to call schools and say, "Would you like me to visit?" Now they all want me to visit. What I do now is try to find a balance to save myself. I don't do the grade schools or the high schools anymore unless it's part of a citywide project or unless I happen to be on tour for some major book and it balances out with visiting a bigger institution. Otherwise I would never be home. Locally, I give back to the institution that is housing my institute; there's a university here that gives us dorm and classroom space for my workshop, which happens once a year. I said, "Well, in turn you could use me as your writer in residence." So when schools want me to visit I say, "In April I'll be reading at Our Lady of the Lake in the afternoon and you can bus your kids to me." I just performed publicly Tuesday night for *Hecho en Tejas*. Plus I do two readings with Macondistas during Macondo, usually on a Friday or a Saturday. As it is, I travel a lot and I am saying yes to the travel. But I am saying yes more to travel to the places where I wanted to go and before couldn't. I would say, "Oh I can't. I'm too busy." Now I'm saying, "What if I die tomorrow? I better go right now." I just came back from Buenos Aires. I'm taking invitations that are scary because I'm afraid of flying—like to New Zealand and Ireland, places that I wouldn't go to alone out of my choice. But if they invite me, then I think I should go there.

NS: *Could you tell us more about the Macondo Writers' workshop that you founded?*

SC: It's a very inclusive place. For me creation isn't separate from spirituality; it's the same, and so to not mention it is a little weird. It's not based on a hierarchy as are patriarchal workshops in the academy; it's a very egalitarian collective. We have a board, but we've been making the decisions on how we grow collectively, and all the writers are invited. They are humbled and put their egos aside; they're people that are writing with a sense of service to the community. We have people that are as young as twenty-three or twenty-four, all the way to professors emeritus in universities. One of the things I learned from organizing the MacArthur "Genius" Grant is that if you mix things up by age and by disciplines, it makes for wonderful creative solutions you wouldn't normally think about. That's another nice thing about Macondo that differentiates us from academic workshops. We might have a performance artist sitting next to an anthropologist sitting next to a screenwriter sitting next to a professor of history. We are only slowly opening the door because it would be a floodgate if we accepted everybody. So we're having to do things on a volunteer basis where everybody pays back. There's no fee except for registration, and that was only recent. Because we are doing things as volunteers, we can only take on so much without the quality going amuck. We want to keep that quality, so we are keeping it small. You have to be invited by another member to come into Macondo. So it really becomes a community—about eighty people come in the summer, and that's a lot for a group of volunteers to work with. We don't have anyone that's full-time yet. That is part of the reason we don't accept open applications. The first job is the writing, and we don't want to be full-time administrators. We would just be overwhelmed, especially since we just had an article in this month's *Poets and Writers*. There's a photo too. The scary thing in the photo is me in costume. I'm in character as Viva Ozuna. I performed Viva's piece about shoplifting from *Caramelo*. Jump Start Theatre creates a whole theme around a guest artist. Last year it was Luis Rodriguez, and his theme was low riders. So we did a whole show with some hip-hop dancers and some low rider cars in front of the theater, but the star was Luis who read his stuff. It was called *Suavecito*, the low rider show from the early seventies.

So I thought, well, what am *I* going to do? I was wearing a Catholic girls' uniform so I wasn't one of those bad girls. It came to me when I was backstage that I was going to wear what I used to wear and be Lala's character with her friend Viva. But this is theater, and backstage is like a Fellini movie, which is one of the reasons I like doing this even though it's crazy to do it on the last night when I've been teaching. The theater hires a professional man, John McBurney, who comes and transforms us. He does theater, he does television, he does movie stars. He lives here in town and travels all over. Backstage you tell him what you want. So I say, "Okay I want to be a chola. I want a ponytail down to there." So he added a big ol' hairpiece, and he did my makeup on down til there [points to neck], blue eye shadow like a painting of John Valdez's. He did the whole number on me, and I turned into Viva Ozuna and realized I am not Lala—I am going to have to do the part from Viva Ozuna!

So they take a picture of me in *Poets and Writers* hugging Angela Kariotis, a Greek writer and a performance artist from New York. Nobody explained to me that they were going to use this photo. I mean I am in character! You look at this photo and I look like a real chola girl. I thought, "Oh my god!"

NS: *It keeps other people guessing about you.*
SC: There is a mythology about me, and I think I've created it. I am part of authoring the bullshit. The persona you create really isn't you when you're a poet or in a performance or a story. It's part of you, but it's parts of everybody, everybody who comes into contact with you. You are like flypaper—you take a little bit of this woman who dances on the table and that one where you know that if you go out with her your clothes will be ruined. You

put it together in an "I" voice and people expect that that's you. All of those voices are me to some degree, and none of them are. So this becomes the mythology. Then you start reading biographies about yourself and you go, "Oh no no no." So now this photo is going to come out in *Poets and Writers*, and people are going to go, "So you see she was a really tough street chick," but that's not me at all. I was the girl with the Catholic uniform.

NS: *And the story grows from there!*
SC: Exactly. It becomes part of the mythology. I make my living going through those truths, and it's wonderful if I fool them, but there's this part of me that people don't realize: that I like to play. I like playacting and dressing up.

NS: *How can people read your work and not know that you like to play? It's in your books.*
SC: I have no idea how they read that and not get it. People who know me know that I am *muy payasa*, very much a clown. I dress up and play. So sometimes when others see this kind of tough girl stance, they think that's not really me, but that's me playing the tough girl, or me pretending to be the ranchera. But it's not me.

EMJ: *Perhaps this desire for play accounts for the humor in your work? How do you manage to keep up the humor in your writing,* Caramelo, *for instance, when there is all this tragedy, all these losses, all these terrible things happening to the family?*
SC: I think humor is a weapon or an antidote to tragedy. If you don't laugh when things are the worst, then you die. You must laugh or else you die. To create something is to stave off your death, it is to stave off the dying of your spirit. Whether you make a poem or a joke or a pie or a song, it's to keep your spirit alive, to nourish it. It's at those times when I am writing from a very dark place that something absurd happens in the writing. I laugh, and then I realize that I'm going to live. If you can laugh, you can survive that day. You have vanquished your foe. It's like wrestling with the angel. You wrestle with the angel when you're going through those deaths or near-deaths, and you are resurrected when you laugh. But I don't set out intending to laugh or say, "Now I am going to write and vanquish that angel of death." No, no, you just really feel terrible, but you have to keep writing,

or you've got a deadline, or life goes on, and so you create something that day, and invariably it will take you to some place you didn't imagine. It astonishes you and makes you laugh. The pieces that are the most tragic parts of the book happened through the most tragic parts of my life in writing the book. Humor comes out in those blackest moments of our lives; the blackest moments in history are when people are most humorous because humor is a form of vanquishing death. Don't you think?

EMJ: *That makes perfect sense.*
SC: I don't *think* this, I just feel things very deeply. When you feel things very deeply, when you're in the lion's den, there is some absurdity to the moment. You have to draw yourself out and look at yourself as a viewer; you're split between it happening to you and viewing yourself, and it's very funny. When you see it from that point of view, you have to laugh because who could imagine you'd be in that situation?

EMJ: *Writing, then, is a performance as well.*
SC: You know, I really am lucky because I have Jump Start literally in my backyard, on the other side of the river. We performed one chapter of *Caramelo* here. See, every year we do a theme depending on who the famoso is. When it was my year, we did a Cabaret de Caramelo, and it was set in a 1950s Mexico City cabaret, and they did all of these performances. So you came into a nightclub—you had to dress in that era if you wanted to—and the actors played bartenders and cigarette girls and emcees, and there was a live band. The company actors did the performances, there was a crooner, Tongolele came out and danced in the spotlight in a tigress bikini, and I came out in this wonderful fifties ball gown that—fortunately you didn't see the back—didn't close. I had long Maria Callas opera-length gloves and my hair done up.

NS: *Another picture for* Poets and Writers!
SC: Yes. This is another persona. I came out like this diva. I did Maria Callas, and I read the chapter that Aunty Light Skin reads about the man whose name no one is allowed to mention [imitates loud music]. I would read a little bit, then there would be a caesura, and another act would come out. Then I would come back [imitates Aunty Light Skin's voice], "And so I was telling you . . . " That's how we did the show. It was great.

EMJ: *What about the part where the Awful Grandmother and Lala are telling the story together? The dialogue that was created collaboratively is a great performance.*

SC: That has never been performed, but that is a great moment where they are playing tug-of-war with the body [laughs]. I felt that was happening when my father was dying. I felt that my grandmother was tugging and I was grabbing my father from the feet. I felt when I was meditating that we were fighting over him. So I decided to invent a scene like that for the book. I was actually living that tug-of-war with my father. I always thought that was a dramatic moment that worked very well. Nobody has done it yet, but I really do think that one day we'll see it in some shape or form. It might not work in theater because it's so big. On the other hand, somebody may astonish me. But I think it would work as a telenovela, then you could do all of the episodes. It would last a year! Why not? It would be like one of those Mexican ones that have a beginning and an end. It wouldn't go on indefinitely.

EMJ: *Something that I find distinctive about* Caramelo *is the history you integrate into the novel. One of my students, an older, nontraditional student who is an educator herself, was talking about this and she said, "I never read this history. We don't get taught this kind of history." When I said, "Let's talk about the Mexican Revolution; what was it about?" there was silence. They didn't know the history. Is literature then a way of getting history?*

SC: They don't know their history because we live in a colonized world. We live in occupied Mexico. One of the reasons why I included so much history in the footnotes is because I feel that we are living in a very imperialistic society, and South Texans, tejanos, are not going to get their history because it would empower them. I think that women are also colonized. I felt that the book was like a Mexican baúl, those lacquered trunks that store rebozos but also store important papers, like the father's shoe box.

EMJ: *Memorializing things?*

SC: It's our time capsules. I know that they weren't going to get this in Texas high schools. It's not going to be on the TAKS.[2] So I always want to educate my readers as much as possible. I also had to educate my editor who is a highly educated, intelligent woman, and when she said, "I don't know who this Empress Carlota is," I said, "Holy smokes, if *she* doesn't know." That's when I gave myself more permission to invent and do things that

I thought were groundbreaking, but I had models for it and that was the footnotes.

NS: *Did you do all of the research yourself or did you have help with it?*
SC: I did the research myself, but I had a young history graduate student to proof it, to make sure that I was right. Actually, there were two young students. Sometimes I would have them run to the library for me. But basically I did the research because I love all that stuff anyway. A lot of the research was done on people, as ethnography, and so I couldn't have gone to the library.

EMJ: *You combine the historical with a wealth of pop culture references.*
SC: Yeah, some of it is the flotsam and jetsam in my brain. I don't know what to do with it. Some of it comes from people I interviewed who would help me get into a certain frame of mind—they're all mentioned in the acknowledgments. People are the walking libraries. I also have my own collections of books because I am very curious about certain themes, and they've come up before, like the Mexican Revolution and Zapata. Those were things I knew. Some things I didn't know that much about and I had to go back and reread. I did read Oscar Lewis's books and testimonios of wars and people in wars and letters from friends that are living in war to help me create the details.

EMJ: *You frequently show women's perspectives, as does Poniatowska in her book* Here's to You, Jesúsa.
SC: Oh, I have never read the whole thing; I've only read trozos, little pieces. I've never read the entire book because I had to read it in Spanish. Maybe that's a mistake because I am so slow in Spanish. I have to read it in English, I have to admit. You give me a book in Spanish and I never get to the end unless it's a novella.

EMJ: *You show a female perspective in "Eyes of Zapata," for instance, which is one of my favorite stories.*
SC: Oh yeah, I didn't *think* that—I *know* that because I lived that woman's perspective, so I was much more interested in his wives. I originally wanted to write it from the point of view of one of the wives. We have all been in love with a Zapata. It's not just the real Zapata, but we all have a Zapata in our lives. I was interested in it because I've had those situations happen to

me, and I thought I could write from what I knew. I *had* to write what I knew, and I didn't know what it was like to be Zapata, but I do know what it is like to be waiting for Zapata to come home.

NS: *When you were growing up in Chicago, Spanish and English were the languages of your home. Were you punished at school for speaking Spanish, as children have been in South Texas?*

SC: I don't know. Maybe they got punished in certain neighborhoods in Chicago. That's very likely. We got punished just for speaking English to each other in the neighborhood I grew up in. We just got punished for being children. We had very unhappy nuns. I like to call them the Order of the Unhappy Housewives of God. Now I have a lot more compassion than then, but we were terrorized just for being children. Well, that was my experience growing up in that kind of an environment where the teacher was always right and you were always wrong.

EMJ: *Were you afraid to be called on?*

SC: Yes, I had that feeling of not wanting to stick out. That was a survival. In my elementary years I just tried to blend in and never to stick out. It was such a vicious place. The memory I have of being in school comes back to me sometimes. I go into elementary schools to speak, there's a certain smell, and I am terrified. I am like Pavlov. I mean I am the guest writer and they don't realize my hands are sweating! I feel like I am being called back to the Mother Superior's office, and here I am about to speak to all these children. If I was Woody Allen, I would just film that shot of me as a little child.

NS: *You do children's voices so well in your books. You have the syntax, you have their language. Do you observe children to get that to work?*

SC: You know, no, I just can't forget it. It's not like I'm taking notes. I do observe children a lot. But that's because I still feel very childlike. I still feel of them. I still feel more like a child than an adult, like a child disguised in adult clothing. So I am much closer to children in some ways, but that doesn't mean I like children. I don't pick up babies and kiss them or put children on my lap. I am not Santa Claus. I feel *like* a child, and one child does not pick up another child. A child is afraid of another child. You know how they say, so and so needs to discover their inner child. I am waiting for the inner adult. That's only kicked in lately since I turned fifty-two, because once I turned fifty, according to the Navajo, you're an adult. At fifty-two, according to other indigenous tribes, you can if you so wish, take on the cloak of an elder. It's a responsibility. But that cloak was put on me at forty when suddenly I came into international prominence and people kept asking me to be a role model. I know I didn't have the wisdom to answer the questions that were thrown at me like huge medicine balls. So I asked in my fortieth year for spiritual growth and boy did I get it. That's what I got in the next ten years, and that was how I wrote *Caramelo*.

NS: *In* Caramelo *you're using more and more Spanish, but you are very sensitive to your world reader. You give hints about what you have just said in Spanish, sometimes in the form of a direct translation. Since you are so scrutinized now, is that inhibiting you from doing something different? Maybe writing more Spanish and not worrying about the person understanding completely?*
SC: You know, I am more concerned now than ever about the Japanese reader. I think about the Japanese reader because I always think, who is the most isolated person on the planet? I think it is the Japanese. When I am writing my book, I think about it being translated into Japanese. I hope that through the context there's enough there that they can get it. They might not get all the jokes, but they'll get the story. I think now beyond the United States. I am thinking more globally when I write my stories.

EMJ: *How do Mexicans react to* Caramelo?
SC: I never went there as an author until last year. Last October was the first time I came face to face with the Mexican public, high school students. I'll be going there in a couple of days at the end of the month to meet with a women's conference. I am astonished. I am only very recently venturing into that realm that I can meet my Mexican public.

EMJ: *Do you work with Mexican writers?*
SC: No, I really feel very separate from them. As I said, I don't read in Spanish very well. I read slowly. I'd much rather read in translation. So no, except for Elena Poniatowska and my friend Claire Joy Smith. I feel very much like I was a daughter in México and went away to the United States, and now I am coming back and meeting my relatives all grown up. That's happening literally and spiritually. I am meeting these people now as an adult. Let me tell you the difference between Mexican and Mexican American writers.

Mexican writers come from a different class. They're upper-class women that have been very privileged and went to school. Mexican American writers, if they went to college, were maybe the first generation. They come from working-class homes, and they are the children of immigrants. That's why our subject matter is very different and we don't know each other.

EMJ: *So much of your work seems to emphasize spaces. There is obviously your much publicized reaction to Bachelard's* Poetics of Space *in* Mango Street. *I just finished rereading* Caramelo, *and there are the internal spaces, the homes, the apartments, the houses, and the urban spaces of Chicago, Mexico City, and San Antonio. What is it about these spaces that intrigues you?*

SC: I think every space either frightens you, makes you ill because you have to clean it, or liberates you. Spaces give you a feeling, no? When I was a child being in a tree was the most magical place I could be; I always felt happy in a tree. I could read there. I had privacy. Nobody could find me. Of course I had to go to the park to get to a tree. In my house there were always a lot of things to do. But my mom was pretty good; if I had a book, that was a pretty good excuse. But I feel as if still I'm very sensitive about ugly spaces or spaces that make me frightened, and there are so many urban spaces that frighten women and children. I felt very frightened in Chicago. Different towns have different emotions for us. Chicago still fills me with fear and dread and sadness every time I go back.

EMJ: *Why is that?*

SC: I just don't feel happy there. If I go to some happy place, I think, "Oh, I wish everyone could come to this part of town," but they're busy in the basement cleaning this building. They're the ones that have to take three busses and a train to get here. Or they have to drive a jollop or spend hours on the expressway to be able to come here, so they're too tired. That's what I think when I am in a beautiful place in Chicago. It's a very disquieting feeling to be there. I just came back from Buenos Aires and I had that same scary feeling. Everyone said, "Watch yourself, be careful." It reminded me of being in Chicago when at any minute you could be happily sitting on a bus, and somebody could get up and machete you just because they are insane—that feeling that anything could happen. It would be a great violation; it could kill you or kill your spirit. It could frighten you at any moment—that has happened to me in Chicago, that feeling that any moment you could be victimized. It's not a pleasant feeling; you can't daydream or imagine or create when you are under that kind of susto. I'm very sensitive about spaces, and I like to create a space even when I'm in a hotel that makes me feel peaceful and happy. That's why in my home and my office I work so hard to make it a refuge for the spirit so I don't have to worry when I get in the car and get out of the car or think about walking from my car to my door. I can think about the stupid things I think about.

EMJ: *When you think of Mexican Chicago, how different is it from Mexican San Antonio? Geographer Daniel Arreola writes that South Texas in particular draws migrants and immigrants from three Mexican states, which creates a relatively homogeneous community. How do you see that?*

SC: Yes, this part of the world reminds me of northern Mexico. It's very much like cowboy country. Cowboy country in Mexico is in the north. But I grew up [in Chicago] with people from the central part, from the valleys, from Michoacán, from Mexico City. There were people from different regions. So if you saw people with the cowboy hats with their names tooled on or with the pointy boots, you would look at them the way that city people look at folks from the country and western tradition, from Nashville. "Who are these country hicks?" There's an attitude of, "Oh, these hillbillies!" It's an attitude that Mexicans have sometimes about other Mexicans, "Oh my god, here we go with the ranchero music and all the cowboy stuff." It's looked at as a very belligerent part of Mexico, the fighting part. So then you look at somebody that is very country the way that people look at Texans or people in the South. They have an attitude of superiority in the North and in the West, don't they? It's like that in Mexico too. Mexicans look at Mexicans from the north, norteños, with the same kind of deprecation.

EMJ: *This reminds me of the soccer match that you describe in* Caramelo. *So Inocencio's attitude towards the other players there transcends his personal perspective.*

SC: Yes. People don't know that. But think about the United States and the regions that dislike each other and the attitudes that cause that. Mexico City people would look at the north and think, "Oh my god, they have no theater there, what are you talking about? They are so uncivilized." I just got that from my cousin who moved to the north, and she couldn't believe that there were no bookstores and no theaters. "They are such barbarians."

EMJ: *My students find it shocking too when they read about Mexican attitudes toward the United States, "What? We are considered barbaric? Us?"*

SC: Gish Jen did that when she wrote her novel *Typical American.* It's about the Chinese immigrants thinking, "What a barbarous country—the typical American is such a rude thing!"

EMJ: *What is Candelaria's background, the little girl who grows up with the Reyes children and whom they see every year in Mexico?*

SC: I have written about the person that Candelaria is based on recently in a post-*Caramelo* essay that hasn't been published yet, so this one is nonfiction. It's called "Natural Daughter," and it's about race and class. I wrote it last year and I've been performing it here and there, but it's still unpublished because I keep adding to it. For the last year and a half I have thought about her a great deal, the real model person.

EMJ: *Amparo, the washerwoman, and her little girl are such objects of derision and condescension on the part of the Awful Grandmother, with attitudes such as "Oh those Indians."*

SC: Oh, that's very very true. I am probably going to read from that essay when I go to Puebla [Mexico] because it just got translated into Spanish by Liliana Valenzuela, my translator friend. I've only read that essay in certain cities—people came up to me and told me secrets about their families and how they were an illegitimate child, and so I think it does carry. I don't know how the Mexican women will take it.

I'm still working on it; there are still themes that are swirling around. For instance, I recently found out that my father was not born the year he said he was, nor the place he said he was. I just found that out a couple of weeks ago, so that's another button for the "Natural Daughter" essay. My birth certificate says that I am white, and that's another button for the essay. These are things that I am thinking about as we redefine ethnicity, and there are differences in the fifty years that I've been on the planet, in the way that my mother was asked to identify herself and the way that we self-identify now—some important things to contemplate.

NS: *When you think about Chicana identity and Chicana writing in the twenty-first century, are there certain expectations tied to that, a certain radicalism, for instance?*

SC: We are all different types of Chicanas; we have very different experiences. We all come from different parts geographically. I don't know Pat [Mora] that well. I know Denise [Chávez] really well, and we can sit down and talk with each other. I know Ruth Behar, the Cuban writer. There are other writers that I am close to. We all do different things. It happened very early on when I was a young writer that I wasn't Chicana enough. People felt that I wasn't writing Chicano poetry because I was writing about love. I wasn't writing Chicano themes. But I always have dealt with my own themes, and I am a Chicana writer and that *is* who I am. I don't have any questions about what I am doing or why I am doing it. It's not an issue. I know who I am. There's always somebody who wants you to be their way of being a Chicana writer. But they don't know me and what I am doing. I do think that the women are very polite and supportive of each other. If we have differences or things that we don't like, we don't say it to each other's faces, unless you happen to be in a workshop. We figure there is enough violence out there that we don't need to. Even if we don't know each other well, there is still a respect and camaraderie.

EMJ: *You said in your disclaimer in* Caramelo *that writing is asking questions. What kinds of questions are you working on now? Can you talk about your most recent projects?*

SC: I'm still adding to this essay about color and race and my father and secrets. I just came back from Buenos Aires and I still haven't put down on paper all of my notes of that trip. I don't know what I feel about that trip. There is a lot floating around that doesn't have language until I write it down. I have a children's book I need to work on. I have poetry that I've been looking to tweak and finish. I have some new things and I have essays that I am working on. So some of these answers, talking about Chicago and its emotions, are the germs for an essay that I can present when I go to Chicago, attitudes about Chicago, possibly for that new introduction [to the anniversary edition of *The House on Mango Street*]. Talking to people will lead to writing essays because I will say something and go, "Well that's right," and then I will go and sit down and then I've got an essay. I've got two different essay projects and several little kettles.

EMJ: *Do you have time to write set aside? Are you very disciplined in terms of your writing?*

SC: No. No, whenever I cannot put on my shoes and leave the house is a good thing. That's when I can do it.

NS: *Can you work in small blocks of time? Or do you need four or five hours?*
SC: Well, I need a block. But I try to do what I can. I've been gone, and you know how it is when you go. I still have two suitcases on the floor and a bag full of receipts and my whole desk is covered.

NS: *Do you have some advice for a student of mine who wants to be a writer? She's thirty years old, the first in her family to go to a university, and her parents are pressuring her, expecting her to get married, which she is resisting. What can she do to get on her path to being a writer?*
SC: I kept putting off children and a marriage because I had other, bigger plans. For a long time in my forties I thought I had to get married to fulfill my father's wish. But when I turned fifty, I realized that I didn't have to get my father's approval anymore. Even though he was spirit, I didn't have to do that. When I was walking down the street a couple of years ago in Havana, a very very dark man with white hair was walking down the street talking to two very dark women with white hair, and he was saying, "No, no es mi novia," she's not my girlfriend, "es l'amor de mi vida."

They giggled, and I giggled too, and I was so glad I happened to be walking down the street at that moment because I realized that's what I want. I don't want a husband; I want a "l'amor de mi vida." So I decided that I was going to have a "l'amor de mi vida" ceremony when I'm fifty-five. The reason why I wanted to get married wasn't that I want to get *married*, I wanted a party and a dress. That's what women want, so why don't we create something where you don't have to get married and can have a big party and the dress and the gifts. So I am going to reinvent it, and I'm going to have a "l'amor de mi vida" ceremony. It's going to be just splendid, all the women that come will dress as "the one" and create their own headdresses, and the men are part of the party. It will be like a circus. It would be like my dream of a Busby Berkeley. I always wanted to jump out of a cake; maybe I'll do this. This is like the whole big party that I never got for my birthday, only better. I asked my partner if he would not marry me, and he said no. And I said, now ask me, and I said no, I won't marry you, so we both agreed that we are going to have this ceremony. It will be a lot of fun.

NS: *And some advice to my student?*

SC: Well, first she has to hang around with writers. You can't become a writer just alone. You must *write* alone. But you've got to have a community. Sometimes that community is on the Internet, and sometimes that community is in the library, in books on the shelf. You have to hang around with writers, whether they are on paper or over cyberspace or in a workshop you go to once in a while, because even though writing is done in solitude, editing is done with your friends. That's how you grow. So you need to keep company with writers in the library, or in the books that are going to lead you to books, or through teachers that will lead you to the books. Also, it's important to have an independent means of income. That means a college degree or several, but it doesn't mean that you have to do your degree in that field, writing. But if you can, do it in some field where it'll support you, where you won't be homeless, where you will have health insurance. You have to understand that you're always going to have two jobs, and you have to remind yourself that your first job is your writing. The second one is your day job.

NS: *When did you get rid of your day job?*

SC: Some writers are very good and never get rid of their day jobs. You should never aspire. If it happens, you are grateful, but you shouldn't wait for it to happen because it never may in your lifetime. That is just the way it is. I mean, me tocó, it was just my luck. There are people who are better writers, and they never lose their day jobs. One percent of writers make their money from their writing. One percent! But for some reason, maybe because my first book [*The House on Mango Street*] is the one that has blurred across borders as to who it's for, it's allowed me to continue writing and to do wonderful things with that book—it's been an amazing journey that first book has taken me to. I meant it for all ages, so it has endured.

Your student just needs to understand that she'll have two jobs and that maybe those two jobs won't allow for children or a partner. They may, but it might be a rather unsympathetic partner who won't like that you have two jobs. And you know what? Get in contact with other writers because she needs to find her spiritual family. Her spiritual family will be who will lead her forward and give her support. That's what Macondo does. We are spiritual families. We are writers who are homeless or whose families don't understand them. You have to find your community, and that's called becoming an adult. It leads you forward and understands you. It is like being gay. You know your family is not going to help you with that, but other gay people will. Writing is like that too, you've got to find your community.

SELECTED WORKS BY SANDRA CISNEROS

Novels
Caramelo. New York: Vintage Books, 2003.
The House on Mango Street. New York: Vintage Books, 1991.

Poetry
Loose Woman. New York: Vintage Books, 1995.
My Wicked Wicked Ways. New York: Turtle Bay Books/Knopf, 1992.

Short Stories
Woman Hollering Creek and Other Stories. New York: Vintage, 1992.

Children's Books
Hairs/Pelitos. New York: Random House, 1997.

Essays
"Cactus Flowers: In Search of Tejana Feminist Poetry." *Third Woman* 3, nos. 1–2 (1986): 73–80.
"From a Writer's Notebook." *The Americas Review* 15, no. 1 (1987): 69–79.
"I Can Live Sola and I Love to Work." *La Voz de Esperanza* (March 1995): 3–6.

NOTES

1. From "Macondo 2007 Highlights" in *La Bloga.* See http://labloga.blogspot.com/2007/08/macondo-2007-highlights.html.
2. Texas Assessment of Knowledge and Skills, a statewide test to measure student performance in grades 3 through 11.

Helena María Viramontes, © Eloy Rodriguez

"YOU CARRY THE BORDER WITH YOU"

Conversation with Helena ᴄMaría Viramontes

In her poetry, short stories, and novels, Helena María Viramontes chronicles the lives of "the despised and the reviled," as Sandra Cisneros notes on the cover of Viramontes's latest novel, Their Dogs Came with Them. *These include illegal border crossers from Central and South American countries, migrant laborers in California's Central Valley, and gang members and the urban dispossessed in East Los Angeles. She views writing as a form of social activism, and language as "a powerful tool for social change."[1] Viramontes captures the realities that frame the lives of these people—uncaring educational institutions, exploitative work conditions employed by agrobusinesses, urban warfare against Latinos and the poor, urban development that leads to the displacement of huge populations, and the criminalization of Mexican Americans. But for Viramontes writing is also "the only way I know how to pray,"[2] and this prayer includes the hopes and dreams of the people, as well as their formation of new and alternate communities.*

Viramontes was born and raised in East Los Angeles as one of eleven children whose father took them to California's Central Valley to pick grapes every summer. She received a BA in English Literature from Immaculate Heart College, where she began writing first poetry, and then fiction. She earned an MFA in Creative Writing from the University of California–Irvine and currently teaches Creative Writing at

Cornell University. Her publications include The Moths and Other Stories *(1985),* Under the Feet of Jesus *(1995), and her most recent novel,* Their Dogs Came with Them *(2007). She also coedited, with María Herrera Sobek, a groundbreaking collection of critical articles,* Chicana Creativity and Criticism: Charting New Frontiers in American Literature *(1987; expanded and revised in 1996). Viramontes was the recipient of an NEA grant and, in 1995, was awarded the Longwood College John Dos Passos Prize for Literature. She was one of six writers chosen to work with Gabriel García Márquez at Robert Redford's Sundance Institute. An activist as well as an author, she also served as editor of the Latino literary and art magazine* XhismeArte.

This interview, conducted at Texas A&M University–Corpus Christi in April of 2007, focuses on Viramontes's literary returns to East Los Angeles as well as on the evolution and long maturation of her latest novel, set in the one-half square mile where her family resided for generations. As she talks about two important preoccupations in her work, the representation of social spaces and historical excavations, Viramontes stresses the writer's responsibility to engage with history. Having thematically linked her latest book to the historical reality of the Conquest, Viramontes proceeds to discuss the results of colonization, evident, for example, in language policy, and manifested in a colonized imagination that deeply affects one's sense of self and that leads to linguistic and cultural insecurities.

EMJ: *Congratulations on the publication this month of* Their Dogs Came with Them. *How long did you work on this novel?*

HMV: Actually this was my first novel because I started it in '91 or '92. I did a couple of drafts of it—I went to Puerto Rico and wrote the second draft in just one month, being completely enclosed and working from five in the morning until about four in the afternoon. I was so tired of doing that that when I came back home I started just reading. You just don't want to write anymore; you want to just read. I was reading Erlinda Gonzales-Berry's *Paletitas de Guayaba.* It's a memoir and she talks about how her father didn't allow her and her sisters to go into a barn. That was really surprising for me, and so I immediately put the book down and thought about it—"Hmmm, why wouldn't a father want the daughter to go into a barn? Oh, because of birth, of the animals having intercourse, of the roll in the hay, of this sexual thing." So I thought, "Okay, why does he have to protect her from her own sexuality?" That's what started the novel [*Under the Feet of Jesus*], and that's why it starts off with a question, "Had they been heading for the barn all along?" I thought it was a short story that would eventually end, and it turned into a longer story. It went from a short story to a long short story to a novella to a novel, and that took about two and a half years. So I really didn't get back to the *Dogs* manuscript until about 1996. My son Francisco found it in my drawer and pulled it out—he must have been between nine and eleven—and he started reading it. He *really* liked it. That's why I dedicated it to him. He would look at me and he'd say, "Mom, this is so good!"

I know he was younger because he was taking a shower and I went to go take towels to him, and he was literally reading the manuscript like this [holds up her hands in gesture of reading] while he was showering because he couldn't put it down. I started laughing. So I told myself maybe there's something there, and I went back to it, and then I just went into it. But working on a university schedule is hard; you work intensely in the summer, you try to work in the fall until you have to quit, and then you just bite your nails until there is more time. I wrote in an essay that writing a novel is not for the fainthearted, but writing it on a university schedule is murderous. It is almost cruel because it takes you weeks just to get back into the blueprint, back into the world, and just when you are back into the world and you have begun the mysterious connecting with the bigger world of this piece, you've got to stop. It's a frustrating thing. So I consider it my first novel, though now it is my second.

EMJ: *You first write about rural California, the Central Valley, in* Under the Feet of Jesus, *documenting the living and working conditions of Mexican American agricultural workers. With* Their Dogs *you return to East L.A., the setting of some of your earlier short stories, and you become a historian of Mexican American experiences in California. What I saw you doing in* Their Dogs *seems similar to what Toni Morrison is doing for Harlem in the 1920s in her novel* Jazz. *You go back to a certain time in history and excavate that history. What was the impetus for going back to that place and that time?*

HMV: I guess it is my little Faulknerian county, my Yoknapatawpha. I find it so fascinating especially in the light of immigration debates—people are always looking at us and saying that we're newly arrived! We're newly arrived?! I am third generation, and really fourth generation in this little parcel in East Los Angeles. My mother was born and raised about a half mile from where she died seventy-eight years later. This half a mile is what intrigues me so much about her living space. So I decided what I want to do is to excavate it. It just captures my imagination. Everything is there: you have the cemeteries and the freeways—two major, *major* metaphors of Los Angeles, and it's all right there on the corner from where I grew up. I was writing about the freeways in *The Moths*, in the story "Neighbors," but I didn't know I was writing about them. I had just mentioned them. It was a scholar, Raúl Villa, who wrote on it and told me, "It is really really interesting that this is in your work," and I thought, "There it is! Absolutely. Are you kidding? There it is." So I decided that I was going to do the excavation of that one-half mile because I felt that I wasn't newly arrived. I've been here for close to four generations!

There are a lot of people like myself in East Los Angeles, and I wanted to record not so much historical fact but the disappeared voices. Where did all these people go from these abandoned neighborhoods? Where did they all go? What happened to them? It's these ghosts that keep pulling me back. It has to do with the freeway and the fact that I left. When I was in Ithaca [New York], I really couldn't write contemporary stories about what was going on in East L.A., but I could write about stories of my memory, and as we know, to a certain extent, memory can be fiction. As soon as you start recalling, you start piecing things together and shaping a story. I couldn't write currently, but I could certainly write honestly about my memory of East Los Angeles. I started doing that and it started opening up all these worlds for me to the point that I don't think that there's a main character in the novel; they all had their stories to tell. That's the other thing I find fascinating, that I couldn't just tell one story. It's impossible for me to just tell one story. I had to tell all these different stories and, like the freeways, have them all intersect. Alevia Rodríguez, a Cuban American poet, heard me read from the manuscript several years ago, and she said, "Helena, you're an exile. You are writing like you are an exile." It made me laugh, and I said, "Well, what do you mean?" She said, "Everything is so minute. Everything is so detailed. That's the way the exile remembers," and I thought, "Well, maybe I do feel like I am in exile in Ithaca, New York!"

The more excavating I do, the more I realize that there is so much more story underneath. At the time I guess my impetus was seeing the bulldozers coming in and literally pulling out the roots of trees. Pulling out *our* roots. That just made me want to go down deeper and deeper. The novel I am working on now is called *The Cemetery Boys*. It starts in 1945 because for me that's a very interesting time. These boys would've had fathers that were in the Second World War. These boys themselves would have to be in the Vietnam War twenty years later. Then I want to jump to 2005. I want to do the parcel of time of my mother's brother and then my oldest brother; that is where I am at now. I cannot get enough of this history of Los Angeles.

EMJ: *Why do you think there is this emphasis on history in recent literature? In Caramelo, Sandra Cisneros gives us all this history of the Mexican Revolution. What is the connection between history and literature?*

HMV: I am not a student of literature, but I can at least say that it is my notion that all great literature at some point or another has to deal with history, has to engage with a particular time. I am not saying that I am trying to write great literature, but I believe profoundly in the fact that writers do have to engage with their historical moment. It's actually the writers who should be giving more of the history than the historians because the writers bring history to life. The historians of course are interested in factual recording. We're not interested in factual recording, we're interested in putting the reader into the moment so that the reader can experience it, and that takes oh so much harder work.

It was very difficult trying to sell the *Dogs* manuscript. They didn't want to buy it because it was very dark. They found it very fascinating, or it was this, that, or the other, but it was just way too dark. Then four editors from New York City wanted to meet me and talk with me. Three of them told me, "No," and one of them said, "It's brilliant. Brilliant. But can you change it?" I said, "I am sorry, I worked on it for ten years; I don't think so. I think I figured every angle out that I could. No, I can't." These editors were literally telling me that nobody in ten years is going to be interested in reading literary books. So finally I told one of the editors, "You know, I think that is just bullshit," and I said, "If you believed that you wouldn't be sitting on your side of the desk."

EMJ: *Of course, he or she is in the wrong job.*

HMV: You know what I mean? But I asked this other editor, "Look, I have been visiting with these editors, and they tell me their thing. How do you feel?" She said, "You know what, people were so stunned by 9/11 that they felt they had to do a lot of self-educating, so right now, nonfiction is just flying off the shelves." I am thinking to myself that that's the writers' call, *we* should be dealing with what we know about 9/11. Why aren't we doing our jobs as writers? Maybe it's us too. We're not engaging, we're not questioning, we're not challenging, we're not screaming, we're not indignant, we're not enraged enough—what's going on here? Maybe something is not right here with us as well. We're not engaging with the historical moments enough. And I think what Sandra did in *Caramelo* was just brilliant. I can *see* the bodies on the floor, I can smell them. She took me to a moment that I have never lived, but I have been able to live it because of her.

EMJ: *That's precisely what* you *do when you take your readers so close to the different voices, the different settings, and the different characters.*
HMV: There were characters that I didn't have any autobiographical models for, and that was a first for me because I had always pulled from my experiences. I guess because you live so far away in exile, you really have to pump your imaginative powers.

EMJ: *In contrast to the way in which L.A. has been written about, as the Sunshine State and with the freeways representing the good life in California, you take us to an East L.A. that is a war zone, with helicopters everywhere, searchlights, and armed police patrols. Was this part of your experience of growing up there?*
HMV: Oh yes, absolutely. In fact, someone questioned the rabies quarantine. I said, "I remember when we had curfews. We felt like criminals. We literally had to stop at points where we were asked where we were going, and what we were doing. We were trying to go into our own homes! Into our own neighborhoods! How do you think that feels?" It feels horrible! So the curfew was accurate, the rabies was not, though. The rabies was something that I made up because I am using the metaphor of the dogs.

EMJ: *Tell us about the dogs and the rabies. The book has an epigraph by Miguel Leon-Portilla that describes the conquistadores arriving with their dogs. Are you suggesting that what went on at that time in L.A. is similar to the Spanish colonization?*
HMV: The impetus of the novel was that I was trying to understand why there was so much brown-on-brown violence. Why are we killing ourselves, and killing ourselves with such brutality? Somebody is killing his enemy's baby sister because he couldn't get to him—such absurdly mean, cruel things. Okay, so how did we become dogs then? If we are treated like dogs, we become dogs. So I had to go back five hundred years to the Conquest and see the way the conquistadores treated the indigenous people. *The Broken*

Spears is an incredible account; these dogs were literally trained to rip flesh. There are etchings of these dogs ripping the flesh of children—children because they were smaller, they were more vulnerable than men and women that could get things and bang the dogs with them. So there was this notion that in order to become a dog, you have to be treated like a dog.

Then I realized that I thought about the freeways as the second conquest with the bulldozers, like landlocked ships coming in here. Basically it was an apocalypto, a real transformation of the neighborhood. Not only do you become an island unto yourself, a quarantine, but you're amputated from the rest of the city. The only way that you even know that you exist is when people pass you. You see this constant motion, but you're completely immobile. It's horrendous. I was telling students recently how the worst kind of colonized imagination is when you hate yourself. When you become your own worst enemy and destroy yourself—that is when colonization is truly effective. That's horrible and cruel, not only for the body, but for the mind as well. That's why in colonization the first thing you want to destroy is the language of another people, the libraries of another people, the artists and the writers, and the intellects of another people. Then you can use the body.

EMJ: *Ben Sáenz writes that when a woman told him, "Your stories are so violent. There is so much sadness," he responded, "I live on the border." What you seem to be implying is that the border is not just the geopolitical border. It's in East L.A., it's in different settings, and violence is part of its essence.*
HMV: Yes, it's the border. When you're treated a certain way, no matter where you go, no matter who you are, you're going to believe that this is the way it has to be. You carry the border with you. You don't have to be near the borderlands to understand that transgression, that violence, in terms of the mind, the heart, and the imagination. Here [in *Their Dogs*] we have these groups of people, like Ermila and her F-troop, who are trying to write stories other than the one, the *only* one that they have. They are trying to write these out; they're imagining other lives. To be able to imagine other lives in a colonized zone is incredibly subversive, and it's incredibly hard to do. That's why the myth of "The People Could Fly" is so beautiful—I love that myth! Having the belief that all you need is a few whispered secret words to be able to escape slavery I'm sure gave the endurance of the spirit to somebody. To believe in that possibility, if only the right person would come and whisper those words! That's why flight is such an important thing in this book. But

it's not a magical realism flight. It is very tied down because slavery was very real. The imagination and the belief though, they are not—that is incredibly powerful. To maintain that during the time of slavery shows a profound beauty of the spirit. That's what I wanted to do in this book, to give those secret words to the reader and let the reader fly. Let's see if the reader decides whether Tranquilina flies or not at the end of the novel. That last paragraph for me is the most important paragraph in the whole book because it took everything before it to get to it.

NS: *It's ambiguous, as is the ending of* Under the Feet of Jesus *with Estrella on the roof of the barn.*
HMV: Yes, very ambiguous. You are absolutely right.

EMJ: *There are also glimpses of forging new communities in this flight, for instance Ana and Tranquilina just take off and start searching for Ben. That is how people survive, isn't it? The community gets destroyed and you have to find something else to replace it.*
HMV: That is why it was so important for me to have Lollie's parents come in. These are parents who love each other; they're raising their family, they're working class, and they're just doing what they have to do to take care of the kids. Then you have Ermila and you have these girls that go, "Yeah, you know, adults are all fucked up," and they're going to take care of themselves. They *have* to take care of themselves. Ermila has this organic consciousness; she is not getting the education in the schools. It all comes from a moral base of some sort that she has, where she is beginning to understand that some things are weird here, some things are unfair here—what is wrong with this picture? She is like Estrella, somebody who is going to just explode somewhere else. I'm very excited for their futures because they are just smart, tough young women. Ben, I don't know where he's at. Tranquilina, I don't know whether she is going to fly or not.

EMJ: *You don't spare your readers but give us some very detailed descriptions of the violence.*
HMV: Well, it exists. What can I say? It was horrible. People throughout the years who've heard me read little sections of it have said, "Why are you writing about gangs? That's so cliché and so passé." I am thinking, "Huh?" Especially in Los Angeles with its 350 different gangs—excuse me? This

takes place in the sixties, though, and there is a difference—now they are just absolutely insane. It doesn't go with the hand-to-hand combat I witnessed.

EMJ: *You manage to make the reader understand Turtle's [a gang member] position. She's doing horrible, violent things, but she is also on drugs and we watch her go, "Oh my god, I am watching myself doing this."*
HMV: Exactly. Also remember she didn't want to get into the car with Santos. If it wasn't for the helicopters coming in for the chase, she wouldn't have. She would have been going back and forth because she wanted this job. Everything was just stacked against her, as it is when you are homeless, as it is when you are incredibly poor. It is a domino effect. Nothing goes right. That's what happened with poor Turtle.

NS: *You were talking earlier about how colonizers attack the language and the culture. In your East Los Angeles household, what did Spanish and English mean for you when you were a child, and how is this reflected in your work?*
HMV: Actually, I spoke about this at the Southern Writers' Convention because somebody asked me about bilingual education. At home, we were all raised to be Spanish speakers. My mother was born in East L.A. and spoke Spanish, even though she went all the way up to the tenth grade at Garfield High, the same high school that I went to. She could read and write in English. My father was primarily a Spanish speaker with only a third-grade education. He went to the same elementary school that I went to, but he was pulled out and never went back to school. He could not read and write too well. So we all grew up with Spanish until we entered the Los Angeles public school system where immediately we were told not to speak Spanish, and my parents, being who they were, thought, "Well okay, it's best that they not speak Spanish." With my mother, for example, we knew that we would speak to her in English and she would respond to us in Spanish. As a result, I can understand Spanish really well, but I can't speak it. There is a whole generation of us who are in the same boat.

NS: *My students regret the fact that they are not able to speak to their grandparents.*
HMV: I'm enraged. I'm indignant with the fact that my language has been stolen from me, not only my Spanish but my indigenous languages as well. I have been censored, and the only language that I have is English right now,

and that infuriates me. It reminds me of a poem by Gustavo Firmat, the Cuban American poet, who says something to the effect that by the very fact that I am telling you this in English, it already falsifies what I am trying to say. Oh, I love that line because it is so true. You do not feel comfortable in English, but do you feel comfortable in a language that has been so far buried that you feel that it is inauthentic to you as well? I am just incensed that I have been censored from my language. I will always remember Cherríe Moraga, who said, "The first five years of my life were nothing but Spanish, and now I have been completely cut off from that person." When you think about it, in the first five years of your life you are creating these images that are associated with the words—how important it is to know that your first introduction to the senses was in Spanish, and then to be ripped from that and taken away! I tried going back and actually taking a Spanish class. But it's very difficult. I don't know if I ever will pass through that psychological barrier.

NS: *However, you do use Spanish in your novels.*
HMV: I have to. These people speak it. I hear them. For example, I am writing about these boys in 1945. When I am going to write about my uncles, which is earlier, I presume that I am going to have to use a lot more Spanish. And when I use more Spanish, I am going to have to refocus my English because I have to contextualize the two languages so that they work out together. In the sixties, for example, there wasn't so much Spanish because we were told not to speak Spanish. We were punished.

NS: *Sandra Cisneros is very sensitive to the non-Spanish-speaking reader. She often translates it or contextualizes the language so that the reader understands exactly what the character is saying. You don't do that, and Benjamin Sáenz says that he won't.*
HMV: Well, Sandra Cisneros is a lot better writer. She and I sat down one time last September, and I was going through her novels, picking out certain phrases and things, and she was explaining them to me. We got to that point where she was saying, "You know, I really want to make a Japanese reader understand what I was saying." I think that is good. It really made me think that maybe I have to do a little bit more of that. I also think to a certain extent that while I don't want to necessarily lose the reader, hell, the reader has got to do some work too.

NS: *Sáenz would agree with you. He says that he's had to put up with this his whole life, and he refuses to accept that "small and mean" viewpoint. If they want to read it, they need to work.*

HMV: Unfortunately, I am such an unconventional writer. The presentation of my two novels is not linear, and I ask a lot of the reader, even in *Under the Feet of Jesus* with the different points of views converging. In *Their Dogs Came with Them* I have over twenty characters; I have all these story lines, I have cross sections, I have this time frame, so I guess I am stuck in the middle, between Ben and Sandra. I want to be sensitive to the reader because I am already demanding them to read a text that's difficult in the first place, so I want to make it a little bit easier for them. At the same time, I do feel that there's a contract between a reader and a writer. This is what Toni Morrison talks about, that the artistic act is not complete until the reader and the writer are actually doing it together. She calls it "the dancing minds," which I love. I want the reader to dance with me, and hell, if I want to be working ten years to give you this piece, please allow me to ask of you to open a dictionary.

Ana Castillo and I had this conversation while we were going to the Zócalo in Mexico City. I was saying that I really would like to write an essay about readership. Not necessarily about the audience—I'm talking about the relationship that I would like to establish with the reader, and I gave her this spiel about "dancing minds," the contract, what have you, and Ana said, "I don't agree with that." She said, "Readers are like lovers, either they love you or they don't." And I said, "But you know you can train lovers [laughs]. You can tell them what you like." I thought it very interesting when she said that it's like chemistry, you either click or you don't. I don't know. With each of the texts, each time we write, we evolve as writers too. So as I am discovering new things about the creative process, about myself, about my characters, about my world, I am hoping that the reader will come in with a willingness to follow.

NS: *How does your process of selecting languages work when you write?*

HMV: With all my heart I say this, and I am not lying, but I am in another world when I am writing. One of the things I've found out, especially with *Their Dogs*, is that I really want to keep myself out of the narrative. I tell myself over and over again, "This work is not about me." I will write from a place that I know of, but it is not about me. So when I'm hearing these characters talk, when I'm hearing these conversations, I have to allow them.

Then I go back and I see whether it sounds authentic or not. Like Ermila when she is talking with her girlfriend—that's from a long time ago. When we were growing up, we didn't have fluid English; our language was a strange kind of mix, and it wasn't all correct. So I tried to make sure that this was the kind of conversation that they had.

The only time that I made a real decision to ensure that everything was understood was in the clinic scene in *Under the Feet of Jesus*. Remember, Petra says something in Spanish and Estrella translates it to the nurse in English again. I felt that it was really utterly important that nothing be missed in that particular scene because of course it was the pivotal scene of the novel, and I just wanted to make sure that nobody didn't get it.

NS: *I'm surprised after reading* Under the Feet of Jesus *that you aren't fluent in Spanish.*

HMV: I speak Spanish but don't feel that I can have a long conversation about anything of substance. I had refused to go to the Sundance Institute with Gabriel García Márquez when I first got invited because he wanted all six of us who were selected to do a presentation in Spanish. At first I thought, "Well, maybe I could do a crash course," but I realized that I couldn't. Then I got upset that I was put in this position. So I said, "No, I'm not going to do it." The woman who was the coordinator at the time asked me why, and I said, "Because historically, Chicanos . . . ," and we went through the whole spiel about the Chicano history, what I told you about having our language stolen, and I said, "So I can understand Spanish but I cannot speak it." She asked, "Are you sure you don't want to?" and I said, "No." Apparently she talked to Gabo and came back to me and said that Gabo understands English real well, but he won't speak it. So I could make my presentation in English and he will talk to me in Spanish. So then I thought, "Oh my god, now I really have to go!" But I said no again. After all, I had my two kids, who were both very young, I had just moved to Nuevo México, I had an NEA, and I was settled down, and I was writing. Then she talked to Gabo again, called me back, and said, "Gabo says to bring the kids." Isn't that incredible! That's when I told Eloy [Rodriguez], "Really, the spirits want me to go."

NS: *So were you happy with your decision to go?*

HMV: Oh yes, was I ever! I must have been nuts, but there was a lot of fear. There was that fear of the language, and there was a fear of him. As it worked out it was a blessed, blessed event. I fell in love with that man. If you read his memoir you see what an incredible guy he is. He's vivacious, he's funny, he's political, he's kind, he's sweet, but he's got his opinions. That's the way he was, like the uncle. Every morning he'd come over and put a cheek out for me to kiss. He'd line up with us to go to lunch, and he'd go, "Sit down, I will serve you," and he would stand in line. He would say, "I can be the most humble with the most humble, but I can be arrogant with the most arrogant." What a sweet man!

EMJ: *Let me get back to what you said about using nonlinear narrative. Where does that originate for you? Is that something that you feel most comfortable with, or is it something that you are more trained in?*

HMV: If you remember, my most famous short story, "The Moths," has a very traditional art to it. It was because I was studying James Joyce's *Dubliners*, and all of his stories have these epiphanies, and then you have the climax, then the resolution, then the conclusion. But one of my favorite novels of course is *Pedro Paramo*. When you read *Pedro Paramo*, you are just astonished; then you read it again and you're astonished again. Then you actually begin to take the pieces and try to put them in a chronological order, and it's beautiful—it fits beautifully, and I think, "Wow, how did he do this?" It is such a masterpiece! I was always interested in the fragmentation of things. That's why I wrote "The Cariboo Café" that way. People have different theories. Paula Moya, for example, thinks that I am a democratic writer, that I'm a writer who doesn't believe in just one story line like the nineteenth-century novelists who had main protagonists, and whose world centered around this main protagonist. I have a world with all of these characters in it. I told Renée Chia from *Poets and Writers* about not having any main characters. She said, "But you know what, Helena, you come from a large family." She said, "I'm a single child so I could see myself very easily writing about one person, one main protagonist. But you have all of these siblings." And I said, "That makes so much sense because I would never favor one sibling over another." So I don't know, Elisabeth, I don't know.

EMJ: *One could also argue that as a historian excavating truth, you are looking at one event, this building of the freeway, from all of these different perspectives, because only that can give you a true picture, if you can ever approximate that. Truth doesn't lie in a single perspective.*

HMV: That makes sense, because there were so many. These people were of great interest to me. Their stories needed to be told, and you wouldn't get them anywhere else. Ana and Ben and the homeless woman—I mean, who writes about the homeless? Then there was Tranquilina, her Mama and Papá Tomás who actually cross the border—all of this. They were just incredible people to me. I also found it interesting that during the time that this was going on, a lot of the teachers in this barrio school were black. I wonder about them not being able to get other jobs. They were very kind with us, they really were very very good. Mrs. Eastman was my sixth-grade teacher.

EMJ: *But grandmother is not so sure about black people, right?*
HMV: She has virtually no interaction with black people except for the teacher. What I wanted to unravel is the way the 1960s were coming up on television. What she sees on TV is so negative, so incredibly racist. After the Watts riot, my mother got petrified. Petrified! She was thinking that they were going to come and kill all of us and burn our houses down because this was what she was seeing on TV. She had no idea. The grandmother feels that she can't protect Ermila, and this is what is so frustrating for her. That's what is making her go a little bit batty. The grandmother is another person that I really like a lot, even though I know she doesn't come off as a very heroic kind of individual.

EMJ: *You write about children a lot and have many child characters in your novels and short stories. What does that allow you to do?*
HMV: What I find interesting is that adolescence is an incredible stage in people's lives. In fact, 60 percent of all first new novels deal with coming of age because it's just such an incredible time. But I also think that children are some of the most vulnerable beings in our society. They have no voice, especially if they are disenfranchised, and they have no one to protect them. I just think they are incredible and that's why I cannot do something without children.

NS: *Estrella's life as a migrant worker could parallel that of a black child working on a white South African farmer's farm, a poor Thai child working for a wealthy landowner—her situation has a global context, but the Spanish in the text situates Estrella in the U.S. and personalizes it. The use of children as laborers in our fields causes a sense of guilt in the reader.*

HMV: That is what is so beautiful about texts that disturb and derail you; that they make you think. It makes you question your own biases, your own reactions, your own values. I love that—I think that's what literature should do. I'm very happy to hear that. Plus, I made a conscious effort not to have the demonic ranchers. Basically, what is it about the family's lives? It is the toil, the heartbreak, the indecency of the labor. I wanted to capture that so that other people could understand and experience it.

EMJ: *These are the things we expect in Sub-Saharan Africa but not here! Not in this country.*
HMV: We have pockets of indentured servants in Alabama and in Florida, where you have undocumented workers who are literally being enslaved and being kept isolated. They're just bodies, working bodies. We always think this country, this country, this country, and this country is one of the biggest hypocrisies of the world.

SELECTED WORKS BY HELENA MARÍA VIRAMONTES

Novels
Under the Feet of Jesus. New York: Plume, 1996.
Their Dogs Came with Them. New York: Atria Books, 2007.

Short Stories
The Moths and Other Stories. Houston: Arte Público Press, 1995.
"Tears on My Pillow." In *New Chicana/Chicano Writing,* edited by Charles M. Tatum, 110–15. Tucson: University of Arizona Press, 1992.

Essays
"The Writes Ofrenda." In *Mascaras,* edited by Lucha Corpi, 125–31. Berkeley: Third Woman Press, 1997.

Anthologies
Chicana Creativity and Criticism: Charting New Frontiers in American Literature, edited by Helena María Viramontes and María Herrera Sobek. Houston: Arte Público Press, 1988. Rpt. Albuquerque: University of New Mexico Press, 1996.
Chicana (W)rites: On Word and Film, edited by María Herrera Sobek and Helena María Viramontes. Berkeley: Third Woman Press, 1995.

NOTES

1. "The Writes Ofrenda," in *Mascaras*, ed. Lucha Corpi (Berkeley: Third Woman Press, 1997), 130.
2. Ibid., 131.

Dagoberto Gilb, courtesy of Ricardo Angel Gilb

"MY GRANDMOTHER MAKES THE BEST TORTILLAS" AND OTHER STEREOTYPES

Conversation with Dagoberto Gilb

Dagoberto Gilb's quickly growing body of work dwells on the lives of working-class people and endows them with a sensitivity of perception and depth of feeling that rashly confronts common stereotypes. His writing critically examines the blueprints American national mythology and popular culture provide of the working poor, of Mexican American men and women, and of Westerners, and thus emphasizes the importance of narrative and storytelling in our lives. Much of his published writing is set in El Paso, where the desert and the mountains are more than backdrop and at times assume the status of fictional characters.

Born to a Mexican mother and a German American father, Gilb grew up in Los Angeles. He graduated from the University of California at Santa Barbara in 1973 with a double major in Philosophy and Religious Studies. After earning a master's degree in Religious Studies, Gilb spent the next sixteen years working as a carpenter on construction sites, mainly in El Paso, Texas, a place he still calls home. During this time he began writing. He is the author of three collections of short stories, the first of which, The Magic of Blood *(1994), won the PEN/Ernest Hemingway Foundation Award, a Jesse Jones Award for best book of fiction from the Texas Institute of Letters, and a Whiting Writer's Award.*

He wrote two novels, The Last Known Residence of Mickey Acuña *(1994), a New York Times notable book of the year, and* The Flowers *(2008). He also published a collection of essays,* Gritos *(2003), which was named finalist for the National Book Critics Circle Award in Criticism. More recently, Gilb compiled an anthology of Texas art and culture, entitled* Hecho en Tejas *(2007). He is the recipient of California's James D. Pheland Award, a Dobie-Paisano Fellowship from the Texas Institute of Letters, a National Endowment for the Arts Fellowship for Creative Writing, as well as a Guggenheim Fellowship. He currently teaches creative writing at Southwest Texas State University in San Marcos.*

We conducted this interview in July 2007 at Gilb's home in Austin, Texas. In it, he addresses this country's perceptions of Mexican Americans in general and of Mexican American writing in particular, drawing on pressures he himself experienced while studying, working, writing, publishing, and teaching. Chicano identities, he shows, are formed through complex processes of negotiation. One of the goals in his writing and in his creation of Hecho *is to break up any homogeneous concept of "Mexican American." Oddly, he thinks, Mexican American literature does not contain many depictions of working-class life. To his students Gilb therefore stresses that "good writing smacks you like a car wreck," and is based on lived, real experiences.*

EMJ: *You must be very proud of your latest publication,* Hecho en Tejas, *a wonderful collection of writing, photography, and artwork. It must have taken you years and years of work.*

DG: No, it didn't take me years and years. I'm kind of tenacious—I go at it. It took about a year and a half, and probably one of its flaws is that there're a few little typos in this first edition that probably come from me driving everybody too hard. It's been quite an experience. I am proud of it, but not in a personal sense. I just think that it's a really valuable book for the community and for Texas and for everybody at large. A lot of people have these stereotypes [of Mexican Americans]—even the literary community has a basic stereotype of what we're supposed to be like. *Hecho* just shows that there is a wide range of people from this color to that color, from this height to that height—Oscar Casares, for instance, is six foot five, and Macarena [Hernández] is about five foot. We are all kinds of people, and we're not just wearing the charro suit or a serape, and we're not all dressing like Frida, and we're not recent immigrants.

NS: *Do you think that's still expected?*
DG: I absolutely do. I'd like to see an exception.

EMJ: *So what made you take on this project? Was it to highlight the diversity of writers?*
DG: Well, in my mind it was. I felt it would be an important thing to do. Plus my own personal story coalesced the more I got into it and saw what everyone else had gone through. I had incredible pressure to publish my first book. I think it's because, even in our community but more so in the larger community, there's a certain stereotype about what can be written about and called Mexican American. They didn't recognize that writing about construction work was part of the culture when, in my opinion, that's a major part of the culture. It's just that you have no writers writing about it; they're all writing about these intellectual political issues, holding banners. I'm writing about people who're looking for jobs and are working. So I had a lot of trouble publishing, because stereotypes held it back. They think that we are all sitting under a Saguaro cactus.

EMJ: *One of the things that is distinctive in your work is your use of the West as a point of reference; not many other Mexican American writers do so. It's there in your settings, in the many allusions to the mythology and cultural practices. How did you develop that perspective?*
DG: I grew up in the West. It's pretty hard to not notice that you are living in the West. The Anglo people I knew were essentially children of cowboy types. The Okies and the Texans and the Mexicans are pretty western even when they are working in factories. They come from pretty rugged backgrounds—it's the old West. They live in the old West *now*. I just came from Iowa where they are living in a bunkhouse. They're living in what would be the turn of the century.

NS: *What are they doing there?*
DG: They're campesinos; they're picking crops. These people need work where they live, and it's basically what the old West would've looked like. But they still live it. That's always been my fascination when people talk about the conditions in the thirties—those are just the Mexicans' condition always! It hasn't changed a bit, but somehow we talk nostalgically about that.

EMJ: *There seems to be a little bit more national coverage of those issues, but still not enough. How do you see the role of the West in the national imagination?*

DG: The West is still ignored by the East—they don't get it. They like it when it is interesting to them—the non-Mexican West is even a stereotype to the East. My *Magic of Blood* book is completely about Mexican Americans, but if you look at the British version you see that the jacket cover is an Airstream trailer. I have no clue where they would have gotten that from inside the book. But they still have certain concepts that they overlay. No matter what we do, they overlay their image. If you ask anybody from California—which is kind of a secondary East Coast—and from New York what Texas looks like, they see the whole state as what the desert outside of El Paso looks like. Anybody who lives here knows that it is extremely lush, green, and humid, but outsiders just don't know. They all think it looks like Arizona, and only Texas would be worse than Arizona.

NS: *It is interesting that you talk about Iowa because when large numbers of Mexican Americans and Mexican immigrants started to move into Iowa, they legislated English as the official language.*

DG: That's the story I was following. On the one hand, everybody wants them, and at the same time there's this fear. I haven't figured this out, and I don't know if I can. I find that most of the panic comes from the people that are not around them much. They love these people, even the guy that owns the farm and is the superintendent of the job site. He goes to a condo in Manzanillo every year in the winter for a month. He doesn't speak a word of Spanish. They're trapped because they have to hire either local Chicanos or Mexicans who are bilingual to deal with the four hundred migrants they bring in on busses. They admire them like every human admires people that work hard, and Mexican people work really hard.

EMJ: *What about the surrounding communities?*

DG: It's hard for me to say. I was in Des Moines and didn't see everything in Iowa, but in Des Moines there is a three- or four-block square that's all Mexican. You see little job ads in Spanish, people obviously looking for illegals to work in the fields. You go to the little Spanish markets that nobody, no Iowan, would even consider driving through. It's an Anglo from Texas who's married to a Mexican who's looking for these people, and he probably had his wife type the ad out. He's the one running the crews.

NS: *It's interesting that we often see official English laws enacted when large numbers of Mexicans or Mexican Americans move into a state. What's your response to those who argue that English is a part of our identity—that we need English to unify the country?*

DG: I think it's just code when they do that. That's what I didn't like about, for instance, Kinky Friedman. Kinky's talk about the borders was just code. You're not really talking about the border when you go, "Well, I talk to Mexicans in San Antonio, and they don't want them [immigrants]." You are talking about a military right wing. San Antonio is a right-wing community, which is very uneducated—a lot of Mexican Americans are undereducated—and they're patriotic and go to the war and think that Republicanism means being strong—that's just a lack of education. But what you're saying is you're supporting the extreme right wing, and that's what the Reagan democrats did. It switched a lot of working people to thinking they can make it too, so a lot of Mexican Americans are just as guilty.

NS: *In California the Mexican American population supported cutting off funding for bilingual education.*

DG: Right. Everybody's confused. But it hasn't stopped in this country. It has never stopped. I read this piece that I am going to try to use some place: "The problem with these people is that they come to the neighborhood, they don't want to learn English, they depress the neighborhood, they bring crime, they have no respect for our laws," a whole list of things like that. It's an English person in Pennsylvania talking about Germans! You read it and go, "My god, that's it, that's what we are hearing now." But it is English people in the 1860s.

NS: *Like what was said about "those damn Irish."*

DG: Yes, that's exactly it. America, very much like George Bush, has a very short frame of what history is. He knows nothing about Iraq, knows nothing about the Middle East, and, in fact, he thinks, "We're better," without understanding any other culture. We just move into your house and say, "Clean your house, you don't need this furniture. You need to do what we're doing." He assumes that these people are not as advanced and skilled in any way, and that's just what's wrong with these people. They think, "We'll teach them democracy." We are a country of two hundred years—never mind it's been five hundred years since the Conquest. That's not very long in the history of

Europe where they are still talking about Rome and Greece. But somehow here, we can't mention that this was Spanish territory. We're in Spain; we are in New Spain; we are in Mexico. Just the other day it was Mexico, and people still don't know why things are called what they are. They have such a short reference frame. In Spain they are completely conscious of the Arabs that were there—the beauty of Spain is basically Arab.

EMJ: *Why do you think that is? We teach at a Hispanic-serving institution where many students don't speak Spanish and don't know what the Mexican Revolution was or when it happened. When speaking about the Conquest, they might comment, "Why keep talking about it? You have to get over it."*

DG: That's not anything really new. "What? Are you bitching about this job? If don't like it, I have ten people that want this job. I can only give you twenty-five hours and no health benefits. You want it or not?" That's where we're at now. I think they've managed to take us back to the turn of the nineteenth century. People don't know what unions are anymore. We've lost all memory of what their value is, and now they manage to make unions sound like something negative—like they're scams, and the corporations are good for not wanting unions. "See, we don't believe in unions," and everyone goes, "Wow, that's great." That's how crazy we have gotten; we've lost everything; we have to start at the beginning. We're in a preindustrial era so we have to teach everyone from the start again.

NS: *So many of our students' parents believed the propaganda being told to them twenty years ago—that Spanish is bad and it is going to hold your child back. As a result, this generation can't talk to their grandparents, and they're having trouble negotiating their two worlds.*

DG: In California, a lot of the Chicano movement comes right out of that. "Here I look at myself, and I look like a Mexican, but I don't feel like one." And yet, the most unique thing about Mexican Americans is that the border is right there. When I grew up there were always Mexicans around, and there were always people who knew no other language [but Spanish], and I was constantly reminded of how much of a pocho I am. That situation is unique, unlike the Germans or the Irish, who were pretty much cut off and within a reasonable amount of time had nothing to do with the old country. The borderland is completely unique. It'll be interesting to see what happens to the Mexicans in New York as New York is going Mexican. Those kids will not be like Chicanos on the border where you are completely linked, no matter what, to that other side some way. Most people have family there, and they grew up with stories of what it was like there.

NS: *New York has a lot of Puerto Ricans that continuously go back and forth.*
DG: I do hear that, but still they are cut off from the movement. So these kids are being told that they are not Mexican Americans because of their English—a lot of Chicanos would have done the same thing to them. I don't agree with that. I just ask, "Is your mother Mexican? Is your father? What do you eat?" There's a point when you've got to get over it and just accept that you are.

NS: *Many Mexicans as well as Mexican Americans tell these kids that they are somehow defective because they don't speak Spanish. But their parents would have been told they were defective if they talked to their children in Spanish.*
DG: Some of this confusion comes more from the Anglo community. A lot of kids who go to good colleges are embarrassed because their Spanish is so bad. But it's precisely because their Spanish is imperfect that they actually made it into a good college. It's a curious thing. All the Anglos expect them to have a cerebellum of Nahuatl and Spanish. Instead of being open and saying, "Look, I don't know any freaking Spanish. My mother is Mexican. Everybody in my life is Mexican, and I came to school here because I speak English," they disguise it. Learn caló, pretend, and put on that serape to disguise who you really are. Maybe they knew a gang member once. Precisely because they are in college is proof that they don't hang out in gangs. But they have to pretend, and they have to put on these disguises, build up their self-respect, appease, and prove that "I am tough, and I am a Chicano." That happened a lot in the early Chicano movement, and it's still there.

NS: *Are your sons [Antonio and Ricardo Gilb] bilingual?*
DG: Not at all, I'm sorry to say. We should have made that better for them.

NS: *When they went away to college did they have to go through these steps?*
DG: My sons didn't. My older son is very much like most kids in El Paso, ashamed of El Paso. He'd say, "My name is Tony." Like most kids they're into Metallica and Nine Inch Nails—the straight long hair, that kind of look—nothing to do with the culture. That is almost evidence that you are

from the Chicano community to me. But my son came to UT [the University of Texas at Austin] and within a few weeks, we're driving around and he says to me, "You know Dad, I'm kind of missing graffiti." He just never realized what it was like to live in an all-white place like Austin. It's very white. He'd never had that experience. The next thing you know, and we never discussed it, he became Antonio. And the next thing I knew he became Antonio Carlos.

My other son, Ricardo, is very smart too. He went to Stanford and just graduated from there. All of his closest and best friends are Chicanos from El Paso. But at Stanford he doesn't discriminate, and on the one hand sometimes you worry about it and then on the other I'm proud of him; he's exactly as he should be. I give him shit all the time. He created a magazine, *Black Ink Review*, and I said, "So where are all the Chicanos? You should put some in." And he said, "I can't find any." So I said, "Well look harder, man. You need to push for it!"

EMJ: *You mention in another interview that you're not fond of mixing politics and literature.*
DG: I think all art is political, but I hate art and literature that just hold up a banner. Take guys crossing the border. It's good, but it's just so obvious. Are we really so dumb that we have to have crayon ideas? "Oh there're five colors and you get to use them." When people talk about the border, for instance, every story is about somebody crossing the desert, which is a real thing, but I know that. I really do understand that already. Give me something new! The border is Los Angeles and Santa Ana, Houston and Dallas.

EMJ: *You do weave into your writing sociopolitical concerns, very subtly—just an offhand comment here and there—regarding environmental racism, lithium in the water supply, racist comments thrown at the characters, poverty, or the waste and the garbage in the yards.*
DG: Right. If you talk to mexicanos themselves, it isn't the biggest subject that they talk about either. The people that are from México do talk about their crossing, but it's not the only story they talk about. The writers have such a limited number of topics that they allow themselves to go into. You know, if there is not a curandero in there . . . come on! If you look at Jewish magazines, they will even say, "No Jewish grandmother stories," because they are so sick of them. That's like my-grandma-makes-the-best-tortillas stories.

None of those! We know that your grandma makes the best tortillas—let's skip it now because we can go farther than that.

EMJ: *Listening to you talk about historical amnesia earlier reminded me of one of your stories, "The Death Mask of Pancho Villa," an icon of international fame whose mask is preserved in Moscow, of all places, and not in Mexico. Is this part of that amnesia? Is it that we don't appreciate the historical monuments in the places where the history happened?*

DG: That's great. That's what I love about literature and being a writer, what you just said. As a writer I had nothing to do with that, but it's true. I don't like the vast majority of what I read precisely because people think things out, and then they decide to make a story around what they've thought out. I find it's always clever and smart and full of shit. But real good stories come from stories that happen. You analyze them after the fact; the story is not exactly how everything happened, but good writing smacks you like a car wreck. You don't know how you're going to feel until it hits you, and you're going to tell it and write it down. Is that a metaphor? You know, you lost your brakes and you rolled into the river. You could metaphorize it.

I'd say that's probably true if I were an English professor reading that story, but it certainly had nothing to do with why I wrote it. I wrote it because there is a death mask. A friend asked me, "Hey, do you want to go see this death mask?" I hang out with this friend who is very much like the character whose name I don't remember in the story. "Hey man, hey Dago, come on over and let's go," he said. He wanted to get stoned and drunk and hang out with this guy, and I didn't. So I recreated it on my front porch and made a story out of these real things that I had discussions about, plus I combined it with real people knocking on my door about similar subjects. I think that is how the art and the craft of writing happens.

EMJ: *Is that how* Mickey Acuña *came about?*

DG: Well, I lived in a Y [YMCA] for too long a time. I don't really like to admit it. In a lot of ways I still live through that kind of thing. I have a certain respect as a construction worker. If I told people then that I went to college, I know that they'd just think that I was a liar. There'd be times when I'd think, "Do I have this self-delusion that I went to college?" Nobody would have any reason to think that I did. For many years I wouldn't talk about it. People would say, "How did you not talk to these people about books and stuff?" Well, at that kind of job it's pretty easy to not talk about books and writing. Nobody ever asks so you never have to bring it up. Although most writers would bring it up because of their big fat egos; they can't help themselves.

NS: *I read that you didn't tell your mother that you were a writer until she was dying.*
DG: Yes, that's sort of sad. I just had a terrible background. It was real nasty, ugly, mean, hostile, and bitter. On the other hand, my mother was on the vanguard of everything. I was just thinking that today as I was driving in. My mother had this advantage that she was beautiful, and that opens everything, so she was always ahead of everybody else. To this day I don't know if she graduated from high school. I realize now that I didn't pursue it because I didn't want to believe it and I didn't want to embarrass her. Not that we had these conversations because I wasn't a conscientious, smart kid—I was more of a troublemaker. Most of our conversations were about the trouble I was in or she was in. One of us was always in some kind of trouble, or we were dealing with something. It wasn't like we reflected!

NS: *You say that you were raised pocho. What was it that made you feel that way?*
DG: As a pocho you don't feel part of the Anglo community, and you don't really feel like a Mexican—your Spanish is lousy, and people are always criticizing the way you talk in English. Much like my mother, who went after rich men, I assumed that rich white girls were more fun. I remember a girlfriend whose mother was ashamed of me, constantly correcting something I'd say. I remember I said "them guys" all the time. It was horrifying to me that I wasn't speaking right. I had no idea that I wasn't speaking right.

NS: *So it wasn't that you were using Spanish words; people just didn't like your grammar?*
DG: Yeah, just the usual broken speech. Also me being unhappy had something to do with it. We went through a really strange period in the sixties and seventies with the Chicanos. I have a weird name so there were always confusions. Sometimes I would be one way and sometimes I would feel the opposite.

NS: *It seems as if you were having trouble figuring out where you belonged.*
DG: My favorite thing was to tell myself that I could be a spy any time I wanted. I was thinking about that recently when I was in Iowa, how my Anglo dad was a super [supervisor], and I worked for him since I was thirteen. No matter whether I was talking in Spanish or talking to black guys, my dad was always mad at me for being too friendly. At the same time I'm sure they must've seen me as the boss's son. So I've always had that thought, that I could achieve shit, and so I could be a boss. At construction sites I'd be a crew boss because not only did I know the work, I could speak Spanish, so I'd get on a Spanish-speaking crew, and have a Spanish-speaking partner. In Iowa one of the interesting but typical things was that most of the crew chiefs and bosses were white people, and I didn't have any trouble with them.

NS: *Because they believed that you were white?*
DG: Yes, exactly. I could just be anything.

EMJ: *Since your writing is so sensitive to place—L.A. and El Paso seem so important—I wonder how living in Austin affects your work?*
DG: I don't know. I'm just starting to put a little Austin in things because it's only been a few years since I realized that I live here. After about seven years I looked up one day and thought, "Oh my god, I really do live here." It was a job place for me, but I don't feel like I'm home. There's nothing to criticize about Austin. I love my office; I actually like this house. But otherwise I always wish I could move the house some place where I like going out. But no, that's not a criticism. Austin people are nice. That's when I worry about me; I'm snippy about things that I shouldn't be snippy about.

EMJ: *Do you miss the desert and the mountains?*
DG: Yes, because it's all real; there's more life as I know it. When I left construction work I had a similar experience and I had to get over that too. It was a momentous experience in that I felt like I wasn't going to be a man anymore. What was I going to do? Hang out with *these* kinds of people? I did it in graduate school, and I hated graduate school. I felt completely alien and did not enjoy any of the classes; I have no friends from there. I had a lot of shame about being Mexican—Mexican being shameful, not smart. I had a lot of issues. When I left construction I thought, "God what should I

do now? If I am around this am I going to lose my manhood?" and I fought that for a while.

There was a point when I didn't like construction, and I remember when this writer friend and I were walking, of all places in Washington, D.C., and I was telling her, "I don't know what I'm supposed to do," and she said something really insightful; she said, "Well, you know the end of *this* story." That was exactly the truth. There was not a single job site that I didn't know already, and there was nothing new happening—I was done with that. Just like when I was in school, I was completely done. I thought, "I don't want to go on; there's nothing that's going to interest me now. I just have to figure out how to get out with the credentials." That was hard because I knew very quickly that this was not what I could be. I thought, "These people are just smarter, they're into things—I can't do it," but I was tenacious—I wanted a master's degree no matter what.

NS: *How does your experience in graduate school affect your teaching now?*
DG: It's awkward because I have to teach creative writing, which is another issue that is difficult because I'm not sure what everybody else is doing. It took me a while to adjust to the feeling that I wasn't cheating people, that they weren't being used. I often don't understand why they're in school. If you want to be a writer, you need to get out of school. Writing isn't about learning these ideas. Talking ideas is a completely different philosophical approach than just having a life to write about. But, I am sometimes wrong. Not everybody is the same.

NS: *Doesn't the classroom give students a community to work in?*
DG: That's what they say. I would have never done it. When I started writing, I was really clumsy, extraordinarily clumsy, it just wasn't me, and I probably would've been criticized. But I never took a class in creative writing. The first things I wrote were terrible, but I didn't know it. Thank god nobody told me. If anybody had, I'd just say, "You know you are just full of shit." I moved forward and within years I could read me and go, "God, that's terrible." But I wouldn't have believed it. It wouldn't have done me any good.

EMJ: *As an instructor, you do get to hear a lot of stories.*
DG: But I don't see that as valuable. Everybody has stories to tell, and you don't have to be educated to have them. Most students don't have that much

life to tell full stories. They're not listening to stories from real people, so they're inventing stories. It's a form of colonialism that I find troublesome. They think that they can imagine anything. No you can't! You can't imagine what it's like to run a five-minute mile—shut up! I resent it. It's like Rush Limbaugh imagining that he knows things about the world. That is just bullshit. It's bullshit when they do it, and it's bullshit when you think you're being good. "Oh, I am going to imagine poverty." So they think of a bedroom that contains twenty-five things, and they think poverty is having five things. You need to live the life, and you need to be honest. They get mad when I say, "No, I don't think men should write from a woman's point of view." The whole point when I read a book is that I want to experience what I can't, and I want the authenticity. What has happened is that so many people don't read anything authentic, they have no idea. I think it has the effect that you elect Bush.

I went to a high school in La Joya, where 99.99 percent are Mexican American kids, mostly bilingual. They all speak English perfectly. We talked to English classes and asked, "Who have you read? What Chicano literature?" Guess who is it? It's Sandra Cisneros. That's the only writer they know.

EMJ: *Not [Rudolfo] Anaya?*
DG: No, that's the generation before; it used to be Anaya. Now it's Sandra, even here. For a year, they study American literature so they can study Steinbeck and all that, but when it comes to Mexican Americans, it's going to be Sandra. I like Sandra, and it's fine to study her, but only her is absolutely crazy. It's very interesting because they think a writer lives in New York. A writer is not somebody that had to go away. They have no idea that writing comes from your feet, from where you live. It's about hearing stories from your grandmother—that really could be literature.

Don Graham, who is the Dobie chair at UT, wrote an anthology called *Literary Austin*, and in an interview about the anthology, he singled me out as saying that my belief that we're not being well represented as literary figures is me being "PC." Meanwhile, *Hecho* didn't get a book review in Austin at publication, but a new John Graves book of criticism got covered on Cinco de Mayo. We had an event here with two hundred people in attendance, and there was no media. If two hundred people buy *Literary Austin*, that'd be pretty impressive. We've sold well into three thousand hardbacks of *Hecho*. Graham's interviewer was saying, "You have included this typically feisty . . . ," which is always me. I always have a jalapeño word next to my name, or a jalapeño adjective to whatever I say. I'm spicy. I'm hot, you know. Linguistically, they are constantly stereotyping too.

Anyway, the interviewer said, "Gilb says you don't pay enough attention to Hispanic literature," and Graham responded, "Gilb is wrong. I do teach this and Gilb is just being politically correct." This is really funny because, first of all, I have never been called politically correct, and second, if you look at the piece that they're referring to, it was written in 1989, almost twenty years ago. It's hilarious because I am talking pretty much exactly as I am talking to you now, and nothing has changed in twenty years, nothing has changed. So he's quoting me from twenty years ago, and I'm only bringing up this story about Rolando Hinojosa and Don Graham teaching completely separate classes. The story is, Don Graham teaches Life and Literature in the Southwest and Rolando Hinojosa has to teach a class called Life and Literature in the Hispanic Southwest, that being the most popular English class at UT. A student taking one doesn't get credit for taking the other. So let's give Don credit that of the fourteen weeks he teaches one week of Mexicans. Can you imagine that Mexican American sitting there in the class? "Oh god, they are talking about me!"

You know, how could you not want to use this book [*Hecho*]? It's just insane! How can you not give us at least two weeks, if not three? This is Texas of all things. It's very curious when you have posters in the school showing a young Chicana graduating with her tassel. Okay, let's just be honest about it and actually have materials that tell that young woman that she comes from a cultural place that has art, music, and talents.

I've learned so many things. I am going to write an essay about Texas for *Granta*. *Granta* did a book that's based on a WPA [Works Progress Administration] project where a different writer from each state wrote a quirky odd piece. They are doing a new version, and I was asked to do Texas. Then a couple of weeks ago the editor wrote me, saying, "You know I'm from Iowa and I was thinking about doing that state, but I think the story in Iowa is its Mexican Americanization, and I was wondering if you wanted to go and we'll pay you a little extra."

Good timing since I'd just finished a novel called *The Flowers*. It's set in an urban environment, and it's about a young boy who's fifteen, representing a story of "coming out," so to speak, in this case as a man. I don't know if I call him a Chicano yet, but he's a Mexican American. He lives in an apartment complex, and it's about all the interactions he has in there. I got the early readers' reactions, and I thought, "God I had no idea that that's what I wrote." So I'm confused about what I wrote now. I guess I have to wait until my own community comes out. But even my own community, and I will say this, is still immature.

NS: *Are you talking about the Chicano community?*
DG: Yes. A lot of the Chicano community is still immature in terms of literature. There is little sophistication in literature or reading. What if I want to talk to you about Beckett or Camus and nobody knows? Well, I don't just want to be talking about Rudy [Anaya] or Sandra [Cisneros]. They're fine but the scope is bigger than just them. I like reading. I like books. I didn't get into this because I wanted to be a politician. I write because I love books and I admire Camus. I like Dostoyevsky. I like Richard Wright.

EMJ: *Is there a little bit of Beckett in* Mickey Acuña?
DG: I hope so. I wouldn't have thought it, and I didn't while I was writing it. But obviously these things come out because you read. And of course I do love Beckett. Who couldn't like Beckett who's read Beckett? There's a little Kerouac, and a little, I'd rather say, García Márquez. I always pick every great Nobel Prize winner when they ask me, "Who influenced you?" My joke is that now that everything is online, if my name is linked to García Márquez and Dostoyevsky and Tolstoy, there I am.

NS: *You asked Rolando Hinojosa who his favorite author was. Who would you say is your favorite?*
DG: That's a good one. Right now, just for the sake of it I'd say Richard Wright. *Native Son* was huge for me. That was a breakout book for me because I had so much anger and confusion in me that the book focused. It worked as both a story and a metaphor, and I liked it. But I'd also pick Lao Tzu, the Chinese philosopher. You know, Chuang Tzu, Plato [laughter]—that's another way of linking to the gods. But I did read them. Lao Tzu did the *Tao Te Ching* and Chuang Tzu is the next level, but he is actually more readable. You should read him because he is just a fun read. He is a Taoist, but he tells really good stories. That's what I loved about philosophy. I loved learning about these cultures and ideas, and I realized the reason I studied philosophy is because I was really messed up. Finally you want to

go to the source. I want to know, finally, where the limit of this is. Instead of hearing, "Okay, yeah, you need a therapist," I needed to find out where that therapist got the information that he's pitching. Finally you get to the bottom and you find out it's Buddha, it's St. Augustine, it's Aquinas, it's Meister Eckhard. There's a handful of people that are basically running the intellectual universe.

NS: *You write in your essay "The Border Trilogy" that when Cormac McCarthy uses Spanish, he is considered literary, but when a Mexican American uses Spanish it's considered irritating. As Mexican American writers become more popular and Spanish is used more widely in books, will its use become more accepted?*
DG: I hope so. My novel has a lot of Spanish in it. It was fascinating because this copyeditor, who I'm sure is a very nice lady, said, "Oh, I am going to help him," for all the right reasons. But it was such an assault on everything, even my dialect, my English. She italicized all the Spanish, whereas Cormac doesn't have to. But I have to explain myself.

NS: *Benjamin Sáenz talked about the same thing. He said that editors want to italicize Spanish but his response is that you italicize foreign languages and this is not a foreign language, it's his language.*
DG: Exactly. But it was not only an assault on that, it was also an assault on my idiomatic use of English. It was a struggle for me. I thought, "Oh my god, if this is what a copyeditor is doing and thinking!" It was exhausting. It took me two weeks to read this manuscript—just five or six pages a day. I was so depressed because they tried to change it, and I had to go back and reverse at least 80 to 90 percent of it.

EMJ: *Did you have to argue with them?*
DG: Oh no. I can do what I want, but I had to pay attention to everything. Of course you always make mistakes and that's what a good copyeditor should catch. But then I got suspicious of every suggestion. I had to think in my head, "How does that sound? Does it change anything?" I have a black character, and the editor even changed some of his dialect, and I thought, "God! This is ridiculous!" To think that it wasn't a willful act on my part, that I don't know what I'm saying or doing at this point is scary. It's definitely there. The worry I have is that if this is how the larger reading population is going to react, then I will never sell. I don't know what to make of it. But it

curiously helps Cormac. It makes him exotic. I actually had a query, "What does hijole mean?" I don't know what to say! What is this? Yiddish is okay. Nobody asks Philip Roth.

NS: *When you are writing, do you edit Spanish in or Spanish out or worry if the reader will understand the text?*
DG: I try to be honest to a voice *and* to be as accommodating as possible. I do think that writing is entertainment, but it's not entertainment like TV or like waterslides—it's intellectual entertainment. I don't want to be pompous, but I do think, "No, you're here." If I go to Germany, I'll read a German book. I want to read a German book and know that I'm getting Germany. And here we are; this is a book set here. Think of a phone call. A phone call transcribed is incredibly boring; it wouldn't be worthy of transcribing. The art of writing good fiction is to make a phone call appear so natural that it doesn't appear like a real phone call, but you think it's a real phone call when you read it. You're supposed to make it seamless. I always feel complimented when people say, "God, I read your story and I think I should be a writer." It means that they think, "Anybody can write," and "I have that story. I have ten of those. It's really really easy." But the disappointing thing is that there's a certain quantity of people that think if it's easy that means I am dumb and not important to read. But my friends keep telling me, "When you're dead, man, everybody is going to like your work!" Yeah, that'll be good for my kids. So I'm glad for myself.

EMJ: *Is there anything else that you would like your readers to know about you?*
DG: Readers! Buy books! People should buy books—skip the pizza and go buy two books. It's a dying industry, and people don't understand that if they don't buy books, we're going to have Bush permanently. If they don't exercise their brains, read something—read the same book every week if you have to, just make your brain function—we'll stay in hell. In college I had to pick areas for my Religious Studies degree, so I decided I'd pick Arabic philosophy. I took two semesters. I was twenty-two or twenty-three and I loved it because it was the history of religion and philosophy and I learned a whole bunch. When 9/11 hit I knew that it was the Wahhabis. The Arabs themselves were scared in the thirties and forties of the same movement in the Pan Arabic world—the Wahhabis were scaring people in Egypt. Radical

fundamentalists were scared of what the Wahhabis would do to the Middle East. So you knew that was an extremist Wahhabi group. Then we go to war and every year the war goes on they say things like, "Oh, you know, they are Shiites." Oh my god! You find out that they didn't know that there are several kinds of Shiites. I am just stunned that they don't know. Nobody sat down with them for a couple of days even? It doesn't seem like Cheney and those people did. I don't think they knew anything about it or they would know that it's historically been a hornet's nest. The whole history of the Wahhabi is anti-Western. They've had horrible problems in the Middle East. They were saying back then what they wish they could do to the British and the United States. You could read it. I had to read in class how they hated coming to America and what it represented. They didn't get that class? This guy wasn't a famous professor!

NS: *If you were conducting this interview, what question would you ask Dago-berto Gilb?*
DG: I just did an interview in Iowa with this woman from Honduras, and it was a curious conversation because she really had the clichés, but it was difficult because in English or even in Spanish she wouldn't understand my humor because she was very serious. So the questions were very serious. Almost every writer that I won't hang out with is pretty much going to answer the question, "Could you tell me what the meaning of life is?" First of all, I think, "God, what a stupid question! You don't ask people that." But worse is when that writer, that person being asked, answers! And I go, "Holy crap!" That's so much the literary business to me. I don't know what I am doing here. I can't stand the people asking and the people answering. I don't know who I think less of. Give me a life. Get me out of here. Let me go back and talk to Mexicans. Así es la vida. You know? I would rather talk to them. They talk about normal things, they talk about their girlfriends, their mothers, everything.

NS: *In one of your interviews you said that when somebody had asked you a literary question you responded, "I don't give a shit about that."*
DG: Yes, they ask these big questions, "If you were to . . . ? How would you change . . . ? How do you know when you are crossing a border?" So I go, "When you see headlights and it's a green SUV, probably you should not cross that border. Don't cross." I get these questions from students—here I

am in a cave and this student's crawling up this cliff, "I am going to find the answer. I am going to find the answer. It's up on the cliff." They pull themselves up, and I am sitting there, and they say, "Master, I have come to find the answer. Can you tell me the meaning of my writing?" And I say, "Fuck you. Get out of my cave." I am making a joke, but in fact that's the truth. Quit asking for people to hold your hand. If you want to go do these things, you've got to go work. Get out of here. You wasted your time coming up to see me and asking me to look at your stuff and sit here with you. If I did that, I wouldn't work. Go to work. Go get a job.

NS: *So how do you deal with these questions?*
DG: Well, I make jokes. It's my only solution. I get these letters from students, from Vista Junior College in Nebraska, and they say, "Dear Dr. Gilb. I am writing a paper on you. And we are reading a story called 'Love in L.A.' I wonder if you can help me with these questions because I need to turn in the paper tomorrow morning. One, what is the setting? Two . . . " It's hysterical. At least here's an honest young person who has the wile to write me this and go, "Hey, I am going to just ask him! He'll give me the right answer—I need a good grade." You know—what's the setting of "Love in L.A."? Ahhhhhh, let me think . . . If you look at that *POV* interview,[1] I think I did it the best there. I was asked some deep questions about the border as a metaphor, and I get to say, "Hey I am hanging a door, should I charge thirty-five or fifty?" I mean if anybody answers that question, don't listen to them.

NS: *Your books have been translated into several languages. Have you done any international readings?*
DG: I have done Germany and France, but I wish I did more. It's interesting that my *Mickey Acuña* book was not well received here. People don't get it, especially the Chicano community. At some point you think, "Well maybe I just didn't do it." I only read it again about a year ago, and I said, "This is the kind of book I like and like to write." But a lot of people don't know Camus, and I'm a little worried about this book that's coming out. A friend told me it wasn't as good as *Mickey Acuña* and I was like, "Hey, thank you." Good news! But the whole Chicano community doesn't like and use it. In Germany, *Mickey Acuña* was reviewed in the best places. After the American tour, my German publisher sent me to all of these places—I was his first

American. I would get questions, and I thought, "If they understand what I did, I didn't just screw up because it's not so subtle."

SELECTED WORKS BY DAGOBERTO GILB

Novels
The Flowers. New York: Grove Press, 2008.
The Last Known Residence of Mickey Acuña. New York: Grove Press, 1994.

Short Stories
The Magic of Blood. New York: Grove Press, 1994.
Winners on the Pass Line. El Paso: Cinco Puntos Press, 1985.
Woodcuts of Women. New York: Grove Press, 2001.

Essays
Gritos: Essays. New York: Grove Press, 2003.

Anthology
Hecho en Tejas: An Anthology of Texas Mexican Literature. Albuquerque: University of New Mexico Press, 2007.

NOTES

1. *POV Border Talk* (2002), http://www.pbs.org/pov/pov2002/borders/talk/dialogue001_dg.html.

Norma Cantú, © Mark Greenburg

TESTIMONIO, RECONNECTION, AND FORGIVENESS

Conversation with Norma Elía Cantú

Laredo, Texas, is the cultural, spiritual, and intellectual nexus of Norma Elía Cantú's work. Born in this South Texas border town, Cantú explores through her fiction, poetry, and nonfiction the area's languages, its stories, its cross-border traditions, and its ways of life. Her work thus provides a distinctively ethnographic perspective of the Texas-Mexico borderlands and captures some of the major cultural shifts that took place there during the twentieth century. It is representative of the ethnographer's desire for recording, for testifying, and for delineating change. Her writing, in both Spanish and English, fuses languages and bridges genres, as does, for example, her first published novel, Canícula, which she self-consciously labels an autobioethnography.

Cantú is a poet, novelist, folklorist, teacher, and administrator who spent much of her life in Laredo. She began her postsecondary education at Laredo Junior College and graduated from Texas A&I University at Laredo (now Texas A&M International University) with a BA in English and a minor in Political Science. She received an MA in English from what is now Texas A&M University–Kingsville, and a Ph.D. from the University of Nebraska–Lincoln, with a dissertation on the Laredo pastorelas (shepherd's plays), supported by a Fulbright

Fellowship to Spain. After graduation, Cantú returned to Laredo to teach at her alma mater while simultaneously working on her writing. She is the author of the award-winning novel Canícula: Snapshots of a Girlhood en la Frontera *(1995), numerous poems, short stories, and essays, and coeditor of anthologies such as* Chicana Traditions: Continuity and Change. *She has completed another novel,* Cabañuelas, *and is currently working on a third piece of fiction, tentatively titled* Champú, or Hair Matters. *Cantú founded and runs the Society for the Study of Gloria Anzaldúa; she is the editor of a book series, Rio Grande/Rio Bravo: Borderlands Culture and Tradition, at Texas A&M University Press; and she has served as a member of the Board of Trustees of the American Folklore Society, the American Folklife Center at the Library of Congress, and the Humanities Texas and the Federation of State Humanities Councils. She currently teaches English at the University of Texas at San Antonio.*

While Laredo is the focal point of Cantú's writing, in this interview she connects what might appear as local and "provincial" matters to national and international affairs, whether it be language attitudes that span from South Texas to Idaho, cultural celebrations that change in their transmission from Mexico to Michigan, musical forms (hip-hop) as a form of resistance in Texas and Spain, or the colonization of the border area by both the United States and Mexico. Having just returned from teaching a summer session in Toledo and characterizing her frequent travels to Spain as a form of forgiveness for the Conquest, she offers a transatlantic perspective on the study of the borderlands. Her final remarks focus on her views of activist scholarship and the much-neglected fact that so much of the work of Chicano/a writers/teachers is a form of scholarly activism. The interview was conducted in Cantú's office on the campus of the University of Texas–San Antonio in July 2007.

EMJ: *First of all, congratulations on receiving the 2007 NACCS, Tejas foco, Premio Letras de Aztlán Award.*
NC: Oh yes. That's really special.

EMJ: *You are both a creative writer and a scholar interested in ethnography and culture. Your dissertation is on the pastorelas, you've worked on the matachines tradition in Northern Mexico and New Mexico, on women's life-cycle rituals, and similar topics. How do you combine those two roles of creative writer and scholar? How do you decide what is going to be a journal article, a poem, a short story, or part of a novel?*

NC: I will give you the smart-ass answer because all writers say, "I don't decide. The work decides for me." It all informs each other. So when I'm doing ethnographic research, I'm really also doing research for the novel. Also, maybe, a poem will be born out of that. It just comes. I don't really set out and say, "Okay, this is going to be a poem." I'll take notes and before I know it, the poem idea is there and it just happens. That's usually how the poetry is born. For example, one thing I never thought I would do is write poems about grammar. I wrote a series of poems not too long ago. In fact, one has already been published on verbs and conjunctions and all kinds of grammatical terms, and I was not setting out to do that. It just came, and I can't even begin to tell you how. I would just be writing and this idea kept creeping up about strong verbs. I thought, "Strong verbs? I haven't thought of strong verbs since I taught grammar." I wrote a poem about strong verbs, and then of course I had to write one about weak verbs, and then conjunctions and prepositions came in, and so I wrote about eight of them for the parts of speech. So I don't choose; the work chooses me. It really is true.

The novel I'm working on right now, and I've been working on it for about two years, is *Champú*. I hope to finish it this summer. It's a story that has been somewhere in the back of my imagination for many many years. It's about a beauty shop because basically that allows me a forum to have women's voices speaking to express all kinds of things, and to also deal with a lot of border issues particular to Laredo—gay bashing, drugs, the violence, immigration. I can discuss all those things from a feminist perspective in a different format than an essay, although I also write essays about these things, but they're different. Both are informed by my own experiences on the border. Well, I never ran a beauty shop, but I was trained as a beautician in Mexico. I went one summer and learned how to do all kinds of things. So I earned money by cutting hair and doing perms and stuff like that, unofficially because I was never licensed. I wanted to use that material somewhere, and so this novel idea has been there for a long time. Ethnographically, I go to salons, and I sit and do my research. I think I am going to come out with an article on the folklore of beauty shops, Chicana beauty shops, because they are different from your regular Anglo or Vietnamese shops. I don't know if you noticed, but all these Vietnamese nail places have little statues, so they have the whole folklore, and I've been toying with an article on those things. That's born out of the research I've done for the novel.

EMJ: *So one feeds into the other?*

NC: Definitely. Both ways.

EMJ: *I heard you read from* Champú *last year, at the University of Texas at Pan American, and there was so much humor in what you read. How do you sustain the humor when you talk about gay bashing or violence?*

NC: Actually, it's not hard to articulate things that are already there. Laredoans, probably all South Texans, love to laugh about their pain. It's part of dealing with, of coping with that pain. There's this very serious, very deeply serious and touching aspect of it. But you make light of it; you joke about things, and it will make it more palatable to live it. The message is stronger in the writing if it has that humor. It's been difficult because before I knew it, there were all of these stories about death. But they were all funny, and I am thinking, "Wait a minute, how can that happen?" I had so many people dying because that is what people would come in and talk about in this beauty shop. Somebody had been killed by mistake coming out of a discotéca in Nuevo Laredo, somebody had died in a car accident, and somebody had died in a train wreck. There were all these deaths, and I thought I'd better do something other than just death stories. So right now I am trying to figure out a sequence—kind of what happed in *Canícula*. I have all these stories and I have to write a sequence that looks like there's no sequence. I'm trying to find a sequence that connects somehow to a climax that I haven't written yet. I don't know where it's going to go. The problem lies in working with narrative that's not linear, with disconnected vignettes, or whatever you want to call them; you have to try to convey some sense of chronology even in that, and that's the design of *Champú*. To answer your questions more specifically, I didn't set out to write a funny book. It's just that the character is so funny, and she finds humor in everything. I have known women like this in Laredo. My mom's comadre who passed away a couple of years ago, Epifania, she just thought everything was funny, and she was always cracking jokes, even in the middle of funerals. There was always something funny in her pain.

EMJ: *On a panel in* Western American Literature *with a number of other writers you say, "I want to talk about my culture and how it's not dead yet."*[1] *You suggest that cultural traditions are alive and change, and I thought about the protagonist in* Canícula *who is like a camera recording. Is that part of what drives you, a desire to preserve?*

NC: Yes definitely, to preserve, chronicle, testify to. A lot of it is testimonio in one way or another, but also, to investigate and theorize through a literary lens, which is not easy. In *Canícula* it has to do with the border reality, but it also has to do with memory and how memory works in a tenuous fashion. We don't always remember things the way we "know" they happened or the way they actually happened. There's a lot of theoretical undergirding to many of the stories that's not apparent. That's not the message I want out there first, but it's inherent in the stories, so a good reader will catch all of that. There is perhaps a didactic note in there of, "This is who I am, this is my culture." But it also makes you think about why people think it is disappearing, why things have changed the way they have, why we must remember, and why we must keep it alive. Culture is a very fluid thing; it changes all the time. There is not one culture. Over time I've observed that particular celebrations, for example the Corpus Christi celebration that we used to have in Laredo, are practically gone. There is a celebration that's liturgical, but it used to be more folk-related. In Toledo, where I was this summer, it's still part of their big popular culture celebration. Why? Well, they value it. Their identity is tied to it.

EMJ: *Has it morphed into something else in Laredo or has it just disappeared?*
NC: It remains in the church but disappeared in its folk aspect. I can't say it's disappeared because it has been absorbed by the liturgical celebration. So my work is about celebrating and affirming as well as, if you don't know any of it, teaching.

EMJ: *I imagine that such aspects of culture become forms of resistance at some point.*
NC: Absolutely, because the forces that would erase it, that would deny it, that would make sure that it does not keep happening, then have to be contended with, for example in the quinceañera. It is probably at its height. Everybody is doing it. For a while it was pretty much gone. Young women were rejecting that cultural aspect and not wanting it. But it's coming back. I think it has come back because a lot of us were very active and celebrating not just our daughters' quinceañeras, but making sure that it happened even if the

young woman did not want it. Then there are the cinquentañera traditions, so that we have this awareness of life markers and their importance in our culture.

EMJ: *What also comes out clearly in your work is the syncretic nature of some of those cultural traditions, the ways in which they absorb aspects from different cultures.*

NC: That is the nature of culture; when you have contact between and among different cultural groups, that's going to happen. The same happens when you have two or more languages interacting, you are going to have a Spanglish of some sort. I just taught a seminar in Spanglish last spring. It was really fun to see the different influences because it is not just Spanish and English, there's also French, and there's German, especially in Texas. We have all these different groups that come in and influence it; it's not just indigenous groups, it's not just Nahuatl, it's also Yaqui and all these other languages getting into that Spanglish that we speak on the border. Culture is similarly shaped by those that are coming in touch with each other. I don't call it a hybrid culture because that implies a biological metaphor that I'm not always happy with. I prefer to think of it as going back to the biological, as an organism, but one that always has a root, and that root is in Mexican/Indian traditions, as well as European traditions grafted onto that, and so in that process you have a new fruit, if you will. On the other hand, it can also be a resistance; some don't want this to happen.

EMJ: *Because people don't want change?*

NC: They don't want change; it's too disturbing to alter the known. It is harder to accept, and usually it's the older generations that resist it. I'm doing some work on huipiles. I've interviewed younger and older women. Generally the older women are the more purist. They don't want huipiles used as seat cushions or aprons. They want to maintain its original function. They don't want to make purses—things that the young people are more amenable to. They think to recycle it in some way is to preserve it. But the more purist are saying no, it's desecration, not preservation. Of course there are some young people also who feel very passionate about not changing things and keeping them and trying to find "authenticity," in quotes, because what's "authentic," right? It's an ever changing criterion.

EMJ: *Driving through the Rio Grande Valley from MacAllen to Raymondsville, one can see how much it has changed in the past few years, with the outlet malls and all-American chain stores often catering to wealthy Mexican tourists along highway 83, a Taqueria Jalisco here and there for local color . . .*

NC: It's colonized from both ways. You mentioned the Taqueria Jalisco. Jalisco is in Mexico, and it is probably an immigrant who came over from Guadalajara and set up a restaurant. But they are all over, literally. Here I counted about twenty Taqueria Jalisco branches. It sounds to me like they're all from Guadalajara. They have a birria, for example, which is not traditional in this area. That's central Mexico. So there is colonization from the two hegemonic forces ongoing culturally in this space where both meet. That's not new. That's been happening for a long time. But the original, if you want to call it that, because Native Americans would have been original, has shifted and changed and yes, the valley is exactly where it is happening, more so than in Laredo in some ways.

EMJ: *As an ethnographer of the border, how do you explain the roles of and attitudes towards Spanish and English in that space? Are they different here in San Antonio?*

NC: Yes, I have noticed the difference. I don't know if it is just numerically—the demographic numbers have shaped the border differently from San Antonio. It's harder to find people who don't speak Spanish in the border areas, even if it is a pocho Spanish; it's more prevalent. Here even the working classes, unless they are recent immigrants, will not speak Spanish. Out of seven students I took with me to Toledo [Spain], only two spoke Spanish. The one was from Laredo and the other one was a recent immigrant whose mother doesn't speak English and came when the student was seven or eight. The racism in San Antonio was so blatant and so severe that it literally erased people's language. There is a whole generation, my generation actually, who would not speak Spanish to their children for fear that they would be punished, discriminated against—things that happened to *them*. They were trying to protect them. Also, I have noticed in San Antonio there are very marked regions of the city that are particularly English-speaking or Spanish-speaking—obviously the west side and the east side. The east side is more African American and the west side is more Mexican. You will have socioeconomic differences, including high crimes rates, health problems, and all that goes along with it. It coincides with the numbers of speakers of Spanish, and I think that is the way the racist system here in the city works. It's still there, although it's changed quite a bit. Whereas in Laredo and in the valley, they did have racism, but it wasn't as prevalent just because of the sheer numbers. If you have 98 percent of the population speaking Spanish at home, it's going to be hard to totally eradicate that. Though we *were* punished. I was hit for speaking Spanish.

EMJ: *Even in Laredo?*
NC: Oh yes. Even in Idaho. I was doing some work up there as part of an art consultant project to look at what the Arts Council could do for Latinos, so we went all over the state and gathered focus groups, and in the evenings when the people were off work they would come. This woman came who really didn't care about the arts. What she wanted to know was what to do about her children's education. I was leading the workshop, and I said, "Sure, tell me what's the problem," and she said, "Well there's two or three things. One, my children won't eat my food anymore. They want pizza and hamburgers; they don't want enchiladas or tacos." We talked about the way that food is a signifier and how the kids are resisting it because they don't want to be identified as Mexican. Then she started crying and said, "What to do about a teacher who is hitting my son for speaking Spanish?" I was shocked. I thought that was forty years ago, but no, it's still happening. The other parents corroborated it, and I was just aghast. There were some non-Mexican people in the room, the Arts Council people, who were shocked and they said, "What?" They were going to talk to board members and do something about that. First of all, it's illegal. You cannot do that. And how can you . . . ? I still think about how my teacher used to do it, and I wonder how she could live with herself, especially since she was Mexican. She was not Anglo! What I have concluded is that she was taught that way, and she thought that was the best way to teach. It was the time of Pavlov's dog and all of that. It was punish and reward, and it was a way of teaching us English.

EMJ: *You yourself learned English at school and then you went home and read Spanish-language romance novels.*
NC: Totally! And still I read a book in Spanish every month. I just finished one that is wonderful; I picked up a whole bunch in Spain.

EMJ: *You also write in Spanish.*
NC: I do but not as much. Poetry more than anything. But I do.

EMJ: *Didn't you write some of* Canícula *in Spanish?*
NC: It is in Spanglish. Then I had to translate it to English, and then I had to translate it to Spanish. Yes. I couldn't find a translator who I thought honored the sentiment of the border, that hybridity that we were talking about. Translating *Canícula* took me a whole summer when I could have been writing *Champú*. It really was an exercise. The temptation was to rewrite it in Spanish. It was very difficult to stick to the text, but I made myself do it. I did delete one piece, and I added another photograph so that the edition in Spanish is slightly different. But it was very hard. I gave a test to about four translators to see what they came up with; it was the first piece on picking cotton, and unless you've done that, you don't have the language in Spanish for it. It was really interesting to see that none of them came out with "zurco" for the row. It was just not in their Spanish vocabulary to use that. They're Chicanas, but they had not done that and didn't have the language for it.

EMJ: *Your story "El Luto" about the relationship between a mother and a daughter is half in English and half in Spanish. The mother speaks only in Spanish and the daughter only in English. This kind of work is very demanding on the reader, and I wonder what obstacles it presents you with in the publishing world.*
NC: You got it. I don't think anyone else, except maybe the *Revista Ventana Abierta*, would have done it. Because Don Luis Leal, who by the way is celebrating his one-hundredth birthday this September, made it a commitment to have a publication that would accept work like mine. He's been wonderful. Where else could I publish that? Invariably they ask you to translate it, either to all Spanish or to all English. But the story wouldn't work the same way. There's another story, "Farewell in Madrid." It's in an online journal in English, and it's published in Spain, in Spanish. The translator did a good job of translating it into Castilian Spanish. But it all hinges on a crossword puzzle and the words in the puzzle. It was very difficult to translate. I am glad I didn't have to do it! But I love to play with language like that.

EMJ: *What audience do you have in mind then?*
NC: I never really think of the audience when I'm writing; I think of the audience when I'm editing. In *Champú*, I am thinking, "Who is going to

read this?" But when I was writing those pieces it was just because! Whatever voice happened to come into the beauty shop. So you have some that are all Spanish, some that are Spanglish. Most of the young people are in English, except for two who are recent immigrants, they are in Spanish. One is trying to learn Spanish, she is forcing herself to. All these voices have different linguistic registers. It is going to be a really hard book to publish. I don't know who is going to take it.

I did another one that is already finished, the one that follows *Canícula*, but I haven't found a publisher for it. This one is called *Cabañuela: A Love Story*. I sent it to New Mexico, which published *Canícula*, and they rejected it and said that it needed to be reworked. I suspect that it was the language, but they didn't say that specifically. They told me some things—that it needed to go in a direction that didn't fit in my view. It is a book divided into nine months—gestation, of course. *Cabañuela* is a way of divining the future based on the month of January so you can tell what's going to happen in the rest of the year. It's like a Farmer's Almanac, that's where the name comes from and that's why the first nine months. It takes place in Madrid in 1980 and in Laredo in 2000. There is a twenty-year gap and it alternates, so it's January in Madrid, January in Laredo, February in Madrid—it's a very complex structure for the novel. I think it works, but obviously the publisher didn't, and I don't know who is going to publish it. I am going to do some more this summer if I have a chance.

EMJ: *What is your connection with Spain?*
NC: I think it's a past life [laughs]. I don't have any other explanation. Growing up, the Spanish were always the bad guys, the bad gachupines, we called them. One of my grandmothers hated them, the other grandmother prided herself in being Spanish. She had blue eyes and a blond family. So the family, my paternal grandparents' family, were very Spanish, although the name Cantú is not Spanish, it's Italian. I don't think my grandfather knew that. It was this inherent battle with the Spanish in me that I think I was trying to overcome. When I got the Fulbright in 1979 and was getting ready to go, my father was very scared for me. He didn't want me to go. He never wanted me to go anywhere. I go back every two years for the Congreso de Literatura Chicana, and that has been a wonderful excuse for going back and connecting with scholars that are doing Chicana literature. Part of my mission in life is to reconnect and to find forgiveness for some of the

atrocities, the awful genocide that happened over five hundred years ago. The Conquest is not over, and it's not over for them either, just like the 1848 war is not over. We still have the vestiges of the violence that we see with police profiling and other things, so we need to also heal that wound that Anzaldúa writes about. It's not a project that ends in five hundred years. It's ongoing. So I think that's where the connection to Spain comes from, from a search to reconcile within me the different violations that have occurred.

EMJ: *Do you find the Spanish receptive?*
NC: Now more than before, much more now than before. In '79/'80 no one had heard of Chicana literature. I was breaking ground. I didn't get too involved with the university folks because I was there doing my research for my dissertation, which was in folklore. But I did come in contact with some writers and some scholars, Luis Cano for example, who were very amenable and open to it, but they really didn't know what it was. Of course, they thought our Spanish was atrocious, but they think everybody's Spanish is atrocious except theirs. So it was a very different climate than we have now. Well, there's this right here [pulls out a book]. It's a dissertation on Anzaldúa and on me, and it's about the border. There are many young women but also some young men working on Chicano/a literature for their dissertations and in their publishing—the short story I told you about was published in a journal in Barcelona, called *Paralelo Sur*, in an issue on Chicano literature. So there is interest, they're doing more work in it. When Sandra Cisneros's *Caramelo* came out, she got a great reception. They really promoted it, did interviews and everything. So I think it is opening up.

EMJ: *Norma González found in her interviews with women on the border that mothers often validate the English language ideology. In her words, the "hegemony of the school is reproduced in and by the consent of well-meaning parents."[2] Do you see that acceptance? If so, do you find acceptance of this ideology problematic?*
NC: Now more so perhaps than when my mother was there, although she validated the English, "Yes, you need to learn." I remember the first day of school when she took me to first grade and dropped me off to this Anglo, English-speaking world, which really wasn't Anglo because my teacher was Rogelia García, who wrote her master's thesis on the folklore of South Texas. I didn't find this out until years later. When I was in her first-grade class, I

just knew that this woman wanted me to speak something I didn't know. She was not the one who punished us, that was another teacher. But my mother said, "Learn everything they teach you." That was her instruction to me. As a very obedient little girl, I took it very seriously. I was learning everything, and I already knew how to read and write in Spanish so it was a little difficult in transitioning to English, but once I picked it up, I went with it. My brothers and sisters didn't have the benefit of being the first child and having a grandmother who taught them to read and write in Spanish. For them it was in some ways easier because they had some English, but it was also more difficult because they didn't have the foundation in Spanish. I think now, like then, the mothers want what's best for their child, whatever it may be and if it's having to have them speak only English, then they'll do that. There's a beautiful poem by Pat Mora—do you know the poem? The mother is saying that she can't talk to her children.

EMJ: *Is it "Elena"?*
NC: Yes. She can't talk to them because they're learning English. I used that poem when I taught literacy, adult literacy, and when teaching mothers English because one of the reasons these mothers were coming to take literacy classes in English was that they wanted to talk to their children. I wanted them to know that they were not alone, that they could learn English, but they shouldn't forget the Spanish. The other thing is that the mainstream culture has negated the value of Spanish so deeply that even the mothers, the parents buy into it. They feel that you can't make it unless you know English, that you have to forget the Spanish to be able to learn English. If it is repeated often enough, people will believe it, and then they start acting on it. Thankfully, my parents both knew some English but refused to speak it. They just didn't. They spoke only Spanish at home.

EMJ: *So Spanish was your main language at home?*
NC: Absolutely, and it still is. My mother was born in Corpus [Christi], so she knows some English. She read *Canícula*. I said, "But mom, you don't know English!" and she said, "But I know the stories." She knew what she was reading. These little things helped me and my siblings keep some of the Spanish. I have to, and I think I've done a good job of forcing myself to learn and to keep it because not everybody can read it. I can't tell you I speak

Spanish at home because I don't. I do Spanglish all over the place. But I read Spanish and I force myself to read Spanish, and that keeps it going. My sister, who is moving here, was reading one of the books I just finished, the one I was telling you about, *La sombra del viento*, and she said, "It's getting easier." When she started reading it, she was hesitant, "I'm not so sure because I hadn't read Spanish in a long time," but as you get into it, like anything else, once you do it often enough it's easy. I think Norma's interviewees are reacting like my mother did—for the good of the child. The difference is that my mother knew that what was good for the child was both. But they believed that what's good is English only.

EMJ: *In one of your pieces in* Canícula, *"Declamación," you say, "Forget contests—too childish, too cursi, too Spanish."[3] What did you mean by "too Spanish," and is that attitude perhaps age-related?*

NC: I think so. It is a teenager thinking that's too "cursi," you don't want to do that, and it's too Spanish because you don't want to be identified with a Mexican American. That happened to me, and I see it with my nephews and nieces. So you reject whatever the home thing is, and of course for us it was Spanish, and also the music. I listened to rock 'n' roll and the Beatles and the Rolling Stones. I never listened to conjunto or mariachi music or any of that, although when we went to weddings, we were dancing to that music. At the same time it was not so much rejecting all of it, because there was Sonny and the Sunliners, and there were the groups that were Chicano but not Mexican. So we rejected more the Mexican but tolerated and bought into the Chicano. The music groups we had in high school played rock 'n' roll, but they also played the normal Chicano stuff which became Tejano. So I have that in-between music, if you will, just like I've had an in-between language, and yet rejecting, as a teenager would, anything that was not American.

EMJ: *So does Nena in* Canícula *when she questions her culture as when she asks why la llorona wants to kill her kid.*

NC: Oh, she's always questioning. Always. Politicians, school, and in "Declamación" she gets up there and does a declamación the way she's been trained, and the teacher says, "No, that's not how you do it." She loses ten points for being late because she has to redo it the right way, so there is this negotiation of the two ways of being and ways of knowing.

EMJ: *So the process of turning your back on whatever is part of your culture becomes part of the process of identity formation, or is this a later process?*
NC: Turning your back on it but at the same time reclaiming it as resistance to that other. I don't know if that's chronological; I think it's recursive. You have situational reactions that elicit a particular resistance. You see this in young kids now with hip-hop. Hip-hop or rap is a huge resistance to the kind of music that I would like, but there'll be another reaction to that. When I tell the students that, they think, "It's not going to happen." One of the students I took with me to Toledo, a doctoral student doing work on hip-hop, found a hip-hop group in Toledo—of course, they do it in Spanish and he's doing it in English, but the music is the same. He found all these resistances. They're all in their twenties and thirties, and they're resisting in similar ways in two different cultures—both are marginalized groups. It's fascinating that that happens, so that's probably a fair assessment of Nena's predicament of trying to resist but at the same time assimilate—I can't even say the word!—so that she becomes acceptable to the school system that's going to reward her assimilation. But at the same time, she retains the home culture that's going to keep her who she is, and that's the identity shifting. Nena wears china poblana, but she also wears cowgirl, so there's these two country signifiers for both Texas and Mexico. We already talked about using both English and Spanish, and she does that too.

EMJ: *Recent discussions of immigration often bring up one of the things you talk about in* Canícula, *the way in which families are interconnected across the border and constantly cross the international bridge back and forth. Texas officials have been saying that the area here is different from Arizona or California in that the ties spread across the geopolitical borders. As culture changes, has this interaction changed as well?*
NC: It has changed, definitely in Laredo because of the violence. It's stopped a lot of the U.S. residents going back to Nuevo Laredo [Mexico] to visit family or just to have dinner. We used to always go across just for entertainment, for dinner and parties—weddings and receptions were held there. Not anymore. Some of the restaurants in Nuevo Laredo have opened up in Laredo because they were losing business. This transnational movement is going both ways. Part of it is the violence, the drug trafficking, and all that. It was there, but it wasn't deadly the way it is now. They had parameters; they would not kill children or women and they would only battle it out

amongst themselves. Now anything goes, so it has really broken down the whole system of social interaction.

Another thing is when a group moves, when they migrate to a new area, they deterritorialize, that is, they lose their grounding. It's not new, it's always happened. It takes a while before it gets established in the new land. In the last twenty years of this process in the United States, from about 1986, which was the last amnesty, there's been a shift. The people that are being deterritorialized in Mexico in this case, for mostly economic reasons, not necessarily political as in previous waves, have come to the United States and rebuilt communities here, pretty much the way they did after the Mexican Revolution. So you have—though they don't call them this—Little Mexicos. Américo Paredes calls it "Greater Mexico," and that whole concept of Greater Mexico informs the ways these cultural expressions develop.

On the other hand, for example, a friend of mine was doing some field work in Michigan, and she asked why the Michoacán community there doesn't do Day of the Dead. This was about ten years ago, and the consultant she was working with said, "Well, our dead are not buried here." Of course it makes all the sense in the world—why would they have a Day of the Dead celebration if there are no dead there? When you start having your dead there, then that cultural tradition comes back, and it has. It's now been documented. There's a beautiful movie by Maria Novarro called *Garden of Eden*. In the movie a community of Mixtecos, an indigenous group from Mexico, come to L.A., and they basically have recreated their community there. But they're still going back to bury their dead, and so there is this constant movement back and forth to practice particular things. Many of the young women go back to Mexico to celebrate their quinceañeras because that's where a lot of the family is, because it's cheaper, or whatever the reason.

EMJ: *Parents send the kids there for the summer.*

NC: Definitely, so that they keep their Spanish. Or it's summer and the parents are working, so they go to the grandparents. That happens, and also the other way. The Mexican population would send kids over here to learn English and then they go back. I don't want to say it's more transnational, but I think there were higher numbers doing that than when I was growing up. I used to go to Monterrey in the summers, but my siblings didn't. Some did, but not everybody did. My cousins used to go to Mexico City with a tía, and now all that has changed.

EMJ: *What is the impact of national policy in the border area?*
NC: Educational policy, No Child Left Behind and testing, of course, is important, but even more apparent is the impact of national policies that impact social welfare because health benefits along the border, as you know, don't compare even to San Antonio. San Antonio has a much larger safety net for indigents for all of those things. It's not what it should be, but it's still there. Of course inner cities in Chicago and Detroit or elsewhere have the same problem as the border. The way that the national policy gets deployed along the border, to use a military term, is different from how it has been deployed elsewhere, in larger cities or in rural America—anything can happen in the rural areas of the country. There is corruption in more ways than we realize, and it hurts us even more severely than we realize. The war on poverty was Lyndon B. Johnson's way of combating poverty in areas like Laredo, where I was a beneficiary. I had a job one summer with Upward Bound. I was in high school with one of these programs, and it helped, but it also did not help enough, or the way it should have.

EMJ: *Some of your early poetry, such as "Unemployed" or "Se me enchina el cuerpo al oír tu cuento," seems very different from your narrative prose—at times starkly realistic and even naturalistic. Does this reflect a more politically engaged side of you?*
NC: That's really interesting because I feel that I am engaged in all of them. That is the voice of "Políticos." Nena's voice in "Políticos" parallels "Se me enchina" or "Unemployed." It's always been there. I don't always publish it for some reason. "Unemployed" is a really early one, and there were a lot of poems like that at the time that I was writing about the social conditions I was seeing. It's probably in the early '70s, '73. There was a whole series of poems that I don't have and I don't know what happened to them—they're all gone. They were about the riots in Mexico City in '68. One of my cousins had been involved in them and was sent to California so he wouldn't have to face the consequences. But many others did. I was in Mexico City at the university in 1972, and the helicopters were hovering with guns pointing down at us and I thought, "Oh my god! What am I getting myself into here?" It scared me, but it also taught me that others are not. Maybe they *are* scared, but they are more courageous than I. I started writing about that because I felt I couldn't be out there doing that.

EMJ: *You said at one point that writing is expiating forgotten demons. What do you mean by that?*

NC: I just confessed to you that I was not courageous enough to be political in the way that I think I should have been, and yet in the writing I am being political and I'm also being honest. Telling the truth is a way of expiating demons, the guilt of not having done something. Or consider this—I never would have worn something low-cut like this because I have bones that stick out. I was so self-conscious about my body that I wouldn't, and I would never take my picture. Between the ages of seventeen and thirty-four, there are no photographs of me, and if there are, they are in family portraits where everybody is there and I had to do it. So what do I do to expiate that demon? I publish a book of poems and photographs about myself. It really was difficult because I had been so private in not wanting those photographs. I don't know if it was about the body or if it was about me spiritually, I have no idea. I'm writing a piece right now for an anthology on spirituality, and I'm calling it "Living la vida santa." It's a Chicana activist spirituality of some kind, but one of the things I was writing about last night is how I didn't choose to have these things happen, they just kind of happened to me. Though probably on a higher level, I did choose them to happen. But consciously I didn't set out to have these things happen, and one of the examples I use is when I was mugged in D.C. when I lived there. It turns out to be one of those epiphanies because I had a very deep spiritual thing happen. While it was happening, of course, I was not thinking that. I was all panicky, and it was a horrible experience. So I am working out a lot of other things through the writing. Writing these stories and writing about spirituality is helping me revisit some of these things and expiate them. The demons are not literal. They're fears, guilt, feelings of insecurity, bad experiences.

EMJ: *There is another set of poems, "Trojan Horse" is one of them, where the speaker compares and yet distances herself from both Helen and Malinche. Or there is "Diosas," which broadens the referential framework to Asian and Middle Eastern goddesses all crying for their children. Do you find any resistance in Chicano/a communities to drawing so heavily on European mythologies and theories as well?*

NC: I haven't yet or at least no one has told me. I do draw on some of that, but I make it mine. I don't know that we can totally disconnect from that since I'm trained in that tradition. I guess that's who I am, just like I'm Spanish as well as indigenous. I can't deny that in my theoretical frame I use a different way of knowing. In "Trojan Horse" I don't just use the European myths, I also bring in Malinche, and in "Diosas," as you noted, it's Gaia and Isis and all of the women goddesses that are crying for what's happened to the women. By the way, "Trojan Horse" is on a wall in South Presa [a street in San Antonio]. I don't know the cross street, but it's across from Torres Taco Haven, you know the restaurant Sandra [Cisneros] talks about?

EMJ: *What a wonderful way to exhibit your work.*
NC: It's the most unusual place I have ever been published! The reason it's on there is that it's a Chicana mural. It's on a laundromat, and all four walls of the building are murals. On one side is Emma Tenayuca and the Pecan Shellers, and there is a corrido; two walls show all these women washing their rebozos, and on the other wall where my poem is, there are four women that are being honored—Lydia Mendoza, Bambi Cárdenas, Manuela Solis Sager, and Maria Berriozabal.⁴ Their portraits are up, and then there is my poem.

EMJ: *I found it interesting to read about your surprise at the reception of* Canícula, *how not only people on the Canadian border identified with the novel, but also African Americans who had picked cotton. We so often relegate certain literature types, Chicana literature, Texas literature, Western literature, to certain regions and populations that reading your comment was refreshing. What does it mean to you that we label literature in this way?*
NC: I think it was Eudora Welty who said something like, "The most regional is the most universal." I'm sure I'm misquoting her, but that was the intent. Not that I am comparing myself to her, but I think whoever writes about a place, any place, is also writing about human beings, and human beings are what make it universal. Obviously it helps if you know the place, if you can identify in that way. I just finished reading *La sombra del viento*—it's been a big hit in Spain and apparently in the U.S. too; it's been translated. It's set in Barcelona. I've been to Barcelona, but I haven't been to all the barrios he mentions or all the streets, and when he names a corner of a street, I don't have a clue. But the story itself, the people, the characters—that's the level where I can connect. But I was surprised, I

didn't expect *Canícula* to resonate the way it has with people, and I'm very thankful and grateful.

EMJ: *How is your work, then, shaped by place? Does it make a difference to you that you don't live in Laredo anymore, that you're now in San Antonio, in a very different environment?*

NC: It does. It's a world away. I drive down, and about twenty miles outside of Laredo when I hit that checkpoint I start feeling it, the love for that place. It's because I was born there. I grew up in Laredo and had been on that border for twenty-six years before I left the first time. I already have my plot, that's where I'm going to be buried, that's where I feel at home. It has to do with the language, it has to do with people saying "pesos" instead of "dollars." We bought a watermelon the other day, and the guy was saying "siete pesos" instead of seven dollars, right? And I thought, "That's so Laredo." People up here don't say that. So there's a palpable difference. Also, San Antonio is a big city. You can go see *La vie en rose*—you couldn't do that in Laredo. I used to come up for movies, drive three hours, see a movie, and drive three hours back on Sundays.

EMJ: *You like the movies? You certainly use many allusions from the movies in your work.*

NC: I love movies. I keep saying that if I hadn't been who I am, I would have been a filmmaker. If I had known I could be a filmmaker, I would have been a filmmaker.

EMJ: *You've already talked about some of the projects you are working on. Is there anything else right now?*

NC: I have so many things going on. Just in terms of books, we are putting together an anthology of Tejana writers; that's been an ongoing project. It's called *Entre Malinche y Guadalupe* because there's a street corner in Laredo that's Malinche and Guadalupe. When I saw what Dagoberto Gilb was doing with *Hecho en Tejas*, I thought, "Oh no," but then I saw that it's totally different. Ours is all women, and it is mostly unpublished pieces from Carmen Tafolla and Pat Mora and others. The other one that's new with Olga [Najera Ramírez] and Brenda Romero is *Dancing Across Borders: Danzas y bailes mexicanos*. Another anthology that I am working on is about Antonio Burciaga, and we wanted it for the anniversary of his death, but it hasn't happened yet.

EMJ: *Is there anything else that you would like your readers to know?*

NC: There are a couple of things. I just did a presentation for our graduate students last fall, and in doing that I realized that there are some things that people don't know about me. Most people know me as a folklorist or as a writer or as a professor. I used to be a teacher who wrote, now I feel that I'm a writer who teaches, and that has been a shift in identity. The folklore is really important to me as well, as you have noted. But there is also the activist work. The presentation I did for the graduate students was called "Scholarly Activism/Activist Scholarship," and I don't think I've consciously spoken about my activism, but it has been there from day one. When I was working in the office at CP&L [Central Power and Light] I was always advocating for women. I didn't have the word for it, but I was being a feminist and being an activist doing the work. Then, even in the poems that you identified, the "Trojan Horse" and many others, there's that tone of resistance that comes from being an activist. In the scholarship there are not many women doing Chicana folklore. Right now we're putting together an encyclopedia of women's folklore and I am on the board—it's a monumental task. I was on the board of the Latino Studies Encyclopedia, and that was a lot of work but we got paid, and that was very different from this one that is a work of love. Right now I am working on a piece about immigration. Somebody else wrote it and didn't have anything on Mexico. It just wasn't on their radar screen. So she is talking about theory and women, folklore and immigration, but it is very esoteric and generic. I want to focus it on Mexico and I am adding a couple of sentences here and there: "For example, when Mexican women . . . ," you know, that is all it takes. But it's not there. So that kind of work is not recognized, and I call it activist scholarship because, had I not been on that board, that never would have been picked up. I think most of us who do this kind of work, María Herrera Sobek is another one, don't ever get acknowledged. We get acknowledged for our own research and for our writing, but not for being at that table insisting that this happen. It takes a lot of energy, it's very laborious, and often it's not recognized. If anything, I would like to say to those out there who read this that we need to be more vocal about it, and we need to recruit more people because we can't do it all.

That was activist scholarship. The scholarly activism is a little different. There I talk about doing work with communities, with cultural centers. As scholars we can contribute in a way that no one else can, not just by documenting, but by working with people to get *them* to document it, and I think that's a very valuable kind of activism. I put together a team to work with the Esperanza Peace and Justice Center here in San Antonio—they asked me if I wanted to help. They needed to do oral histories for a project where they were collecting old photographs from the community. I said, "Yeah I'll help, but I'm not going to do it. I want to help you train people from that community to do it." So I recruited two other colleagues here at the university, Dennis Medina and Lisa de la Portilla, and we did a workshop, and those people did the research. That's a much more effective way of getting to it, instead of me going there and telling them what to do and how to do it. That kind of activism I don't think is acknowledged, or people don't know about it. I don't write about it.

The other thing about the writing that I don't think we talked about is the difficulty in finding time to do it. It really is serious for those of us that have jobs and write just to carve out the time to do it. I have to write. Even if I am falling asleep, I write in my journal or I write something—I have to do it, and it's hard if you don't have the time. I do too many things and am multitasking all the time. I think it comes from being the oldest. Almost like a mother of ten, right? You have to organize it so things happen, even though it doesn't look like it's organized. Things get done.

SELECTED WORKS BY NORMA ELÍA CANTÚ

Novel
Canícula: Snapshots of a Girlhood en la frontera. Albuquerque: University of New Mexico Press, 1997.

Poetry
"Border Bullets," "My Body/The Body," and "Meditación Fronteriza." *Chicana/Latina Studies: The Journal of Mujeres Activas en Letras y Cambio Social* 6, no. 1 (2006): 90–94.
"Decolonizing the Mind" and "Trojan Horse." In *Floricanto Sí: A Collection of U.S. Latina Poetry,* edited by Bryce Milligan and Angela De Hoyos, 44. New York: Penguin, 1998.
"Diosas" and "Fiestas de diciembre." *Blue Mesa Review* 9 (1997): 71–75.
"Se me enchina el cuerpo al oír tu cuento." In *New Chicano/a Writing,* edited by Charles M. Tatum, 101–2. Tucson: University of Arizona Press, 1992.
"Unemployed." *Huehuetitlan* 3&4 (1984): 2.
"Untitled." *Huehuetitlan* (1983).

Short Story
"El luto." *Ventana Abierta: Revista latina de literatura, arte y cultura* 1, no. 4 (1998): 46–51.

Anthologies
Chicana Traditions: Continuity and Change, edited by Norma Cantú and Olga Nájera Ramírez. Urbana: University of Illinois Press, 2002.
Flor y Ciencia: Chicanas in Mathematics, Science, and Engineering. American Association for the Advancement of Science Adelante Project, 2006.
Telling to Live: Latina Feminist Testimonios. With Latina Feminist Group. Durham: Duke University Press, 2001.

Essays
"Bailando y Cantando," in *Blue Mesa Review* 9, edited by David M. Johnson. Albuquerque: University of New Mexico Press, 1997.
"Capirotada: A Lenten Treat." In *Stirring Prose: Cooking with Texas Authors,* edited by Deborah Douglas, 42–45. College Station: Texas A&M University Press, 1998.
"Chicana Life-Cycle Rituals." In *Chicana Traditions: Continuity and Change,* edited by Norma Cantú and Olga Nájera Ramírez, 15–34. Urbana: University of Illinois Press, 2002.
"Costume as Cultural Resistance and Affirmation: The Case of a South Texas Community." In *Hecho en Tejas: Texas-Mexican Folk Arts and Crafts,* edited by Joe S. Graham, 117–30. Denton: University of North Texas Press, 1992.
"Getting There *Cuando No Hay Camino.*" Cantú and Latina Feminist Group, 60–68.
"Los Matachines de la Santa Cruz de la Ladrillera: Notes Toward a Socio-Literary Analysis." In *Feasts and Celebrations in U.S. Ethnic Communities,* edited by Ramón Gutierrez, 57–67. Albuquerque: University of New Mexico Press, 1995.
"The Mexican-American Quilting Traditions of Laredo, San Ygnacio and Zapata." Co-authored with Ofelia Zapata Vela. In *Hecho en Tejas: Texas-Mexican Folk Arts and Crafts,* edited by Joe S. Graham, 77–92. Denton: University of North Texas Press, 1992.
"Pastoras and Malinches: Women in a Traditional Folk Drama of Laredo, Texas." *Recovering the U.S. Literary Heritage Project,* 172–83. Houston: Arte Público Press, 2003.
"La Quinceañera: Towards an Ethnographic Analysis of a Life-Cycle Ritual." *Southern Folklore* 56, no. 1 (1999): 73–101.
"La Virgen de Guadalupe: Symbol of Faith and Devotion." *Familia, Fé y Fiestas/Family, Faith and Fiestas: Mexican American Celebrations of the Holiday Season.* Arte Americas and Fresno Arts Council, 1996.

NOTES

1. Kathleen Boardman, "Western Autobiography and Memoir: A Panel of Writers," *Western American Literature Special Issue: Western Autobiography and Memoir* 37, no. 2 (2002): 163.

2. Norma González, *I Am My Language: Discourses of Women and Children in the Border-lands* (Tucson: University of Arizona Press, 2001), 165.

3. *Canícula: Snapshots of a Girlhood en la frontera* (Albuquerque: University of New Mexico Press, 1997), 63.

4. Tenayuca was a political activist who led the Pecan Shellers strike in 1938. A mural by artist and activist Terry Ybáñez honors her memory. Lydia Mendoza is also known as the "Queen of Tejano," famous for singing in the plazas of San Antonio in the 1930s. Bambi Cárdenas is an educational leader and civil rights advocate who currently serves as the first female president of the University of Texas–Pan American. Manuela Soliz Sager was a leader in the Mexican American labor movement from the 1930s onward. Maria Antonietta Berriozabal is a community activist who founded Hispanas Unidas in San Antonio in 1983. The group is dedicated to the advancement of Hispanic women.

Denise Chávez, © Daniel Zolinsky

"¡AY, EL INGLÉS TAN BONITO!"

Conversation with Denise Chávez

Denise Chávez's works come out of the rich tradition of nueva mexicanas writing about their culture. Like Fabiola Cabeza de Baca Gilbert, whose The Good Life: New Mexico Food and Traditions *(1949) features stories about a family in an isolated New Mexican village, Chávez sets much of her work in the small towns in rural New Mexico. She traces the lives of women who seek to rid themselves of the shackles of inhibiting gender roles, who attempt to live meaningful lives without men, and who, in the process of trying to reach independence, forge new female communities. The hallmark of Chávez's work is its quilt-like structure, consisting of multiple and often clashing voices out of which the author, like the quilt maker, creates an object of aesthetic value. Her storytelling blends the genres of testimonio (the narrative of witnessing), memoir (celebrating common people and elevating them from their everyday existence), and ethnography. It is at the same time a culinary journey, connecting food to culture and memory.*

Chávez is a playwright, novelist, short story writer, actor, educator, and activist, who was raised in Las Cruces, New Mexico. She received a BA in Drama from New Mexico State University, an MFA in Drama from Trinity University, and an MA in Creative Writing from the University of New Mexico. Her love of the theater is well represented in her over forty-five plays including Plague-Time

(1985), Novena narrativas *(1986), and* The Last of the Menu Girls *(1986), which was adapted from her short stories of the same title published in 1986. She has written two novels,* Face of an Angel *(1994) and* Loving Pedro Infante *(2001), and a memoir of family and food,* A Taco Testimony *(2006). She has received numerous awards for both her public service and her writing. Among her service awards are the 2004 Governor's New Mexico Distinguished Public Service Award, the 1998 Papen Family Arts Award for service and leadership in the Las Cruces Area, and the Luminaria Award for Community Service, New Mexico Community Foundation (1996). Her numerous literary awards include the Don Luis Leal award in Chicano Literature (2005), the Hispanic Heritage Award Honoree in Literature (2004), the Literary Award (2004) from the National Hispanic Cultural Center in Albuquerque, New Mexico, and the New Mexico Governor's Award in Literature (1995).* Face of an Angel *won the Premio Aztlán Award, the American Book Award, and the Mesilla Valley Writer of the Year Award, all in 1995. She was the recipient of a Lila Wallace–Reader's Digest Fellowship and a Rockefeller Foundation grant; she has also traveled to universities in Spain as a Fulbright Senior Specialist in Chicano Literature. She has performed her one-woman shows,* Women in the State of Grace *and* El Muro/The Wall, *throughout the United States. Chávez has been the Executive Director of the Border Book Festival, an annual celebration of the arts in the borderlands featuring local, national, and international artists, since its inception in 1994. She is also the founder of the Cultural Center de Mesilla, an arts resource center, workshop, and performance venue, and home of the Border Book Festival.*

We met Chávez in March 2008, at Texas A&M University–Corpus Christi during her visit to the campus. In this interview, Chávez explains how she grew up surrounded by stories. She claims that growing up with a tradition of storytelling and subsequently receiving training in theater significantly shaped her writing. Throughout her conversation, she conveys a sense of enthusiasm and commitment for her work to improve life in the community in which she lives, Mesilla, New Mexico. "If we can heal the border, we can heal the world," Chávez declares. She argues very strongly for adopting a global view to the borderlands, citing the linguistic and cultural diversity of the populations on the New Mexico/ Texas/México border and stressing the day-to-day interactions among the people that populate this area.

EMJ: *Mama Lupita, the protagonist's grandmother, says in* Face of an Angel: *"Everyone has a story."[1] Your novels have a huge cast of characters, many different voices, and embedded stories. There is a distinctly oral quality to the texts. What is it about storytelling that intrigues you?*

DC: I grew up with stories. My mother was a wonderful storyteller and so was my father. When you come from that oral tradition, listening to stories is very important—sitting around the dinner table or, as in the *Taco Testimony*, sitting around the taco table, sitting outside in the backyard eating sandía, watermelon, in the summertime, or going to my mother's home in far west Texas. There wasn't much out in the polvo, the dust, in Redford, Texas. My aunt had an incredible library, and so our entertainment was the stories and the books. That's what we did during the day when it was so hot and you wouldn't go out; you would read, read, read. We were all incredible readers and we loved stories. We loved visiting with people; our life was spent circulating amongst family. My mother was always talking about her tío Irineo. I have glorified him in various ways throughout my writing. He had incredible adventures. He was the person that went into a cave and fell asleep and woke up with a rattler on his stomach. This man reached mythic proportions. He was fabulous. My mother's great-grandfather, Nabor, who came and settled El Polvo, was a man of mystery. His father had been kidnapped by Apaches and he returned to this part of the world as a young man. He was the person that used to go out every morning to salute the sun. He was Native American in his lifestyle. I grew up with this tapestry of stories, and this tapestry was my shawl, my solace; it was everything that I was, and I learned from the best storytellers.

EMJ: *Why do the stories start with the men and end with the women? Is it because the men were the immigrants?*

DC: Well, no because they were the ones that ruled in the traditional Hispano family, even my father, who was a very weak person in many ways—he was an alcoholic for seventy whatever years. They begin with the men because we come from a tradition in which men were first and foremost. In my particular family, my father, his well-being, his ups and downs ruled our lives. They begin with the men because we're a traditional culture in which everything was relegated to my father's happiness. Is he okay? Is he coming back? Does he need anything? The mothers supported this too. "Come on mijito, come have something to eat." Even if the son comes in at two a.m. from the bar, there's the mother fixing him food, cleaning him up. I haven't thought of the immigrant aspect because the women have certainly been as strong as the men, stronger than the men. However, there was that façade, that patina, the illusion that the men were in charge when in fact they were and they weren't. But in that day and age and in that generation, that's what you were given, that was the face that you were given. You were a woman.

EMJ: *Going back to the storytelling, you're not just telling the stories for the sake of storytelling. In one piece that you have about writing, you say that you are writing for the poor and the forgotten. So is part of it recording the lives of the poor and the forgotten?*

DC: I think so—transmuting, reporting. I always think that writers are taking from the spirit world. We're transmuting voices. I was in Edinburgh at Pan American [Texas A&M University–Pan American] for a writers' conference, and one of the students asked me, "Why do you write?" I gave him my description that I had written some years back. I said I write to set the spirits in motion to be freed, and honestly that's how I feel. Writing is a healing act, a transformative act, and so I feel that I am not only working on my spirits, but spirits of the world to set them in motion to be freed because I have a very spiritual nature. I grew up Catholic; I have Jewish roots in México— sephardita roots in el estado de Chihuahua—but I am also Buddhist in my thinking, and like Thich Nhat Hanh, I believe you can go back to the past and heal the present. He says with great understanding, one can visit the past and go back there and heal, and I really believe that. *Taco Testimony*, my latest book, is the most personal thing I've written, although I've written many, many personal things.

A lot of the stories that I'm gathering now for a collection of short cuentitos are very, very personal. *El Inglés Tan Bonito, Beautiful English* I call it, and this is from my grandmother, Antonia Luján. She traveled across the U.S. with a settler family in a covered wagon, and she learned English with them. She felt that to be able to have two languages was the beginning of a lot of her power. She always said, "Ay, el Inglés tan bonito," which is really the opposite of what one would imagine. English *is* beautiful. People don't think of English as a beautiful language, but to her it was a beautiful and powerful language. That is why her children went on to graduate from Sul Ross University, why they have that inverted R—they have the brands of the settler families on the campus. To her that meant something. That is what I feel. Writing is here to transform, to heal, to empower, to enlighten, and to manifest possibility for people.

EMJ: *To preserve culture as well? I'm thinking of Oralia in* Face of an Angel, *for instance. She is such a great character, the guardian of culture. What happens when her generation dies out?*

DC: It will never die out. Yes, there may be a diminishing sense, but at the same time, there are many people that are keeping culture alive, and I see them all the time. We have coming to our book festival Cipriano Vigil, who played at the Smithsonian. He's a músico, but he's also a writer. He's singing with his son, Cipriano Jr., and his daughter. They're La Familia Vigil. These are people that are keeping things alive. I honestly believe that. I don't have children; my children are my books. But there are people that are teaching their children to speak dual languages, to appreciate the multicultural landscapes. I'm very enthusiastic about the topic of your book. I believe if we can heal the border, we heal the world because we are the border. Borders are us, and global identity is how we need to think right now. I feel that I need to be working on a playing field that reaches Latin America, México, different places in the world.

Not only do we have a book festival in April, but now we're running a little bookstore, an art center, and a cultural center, which I founded about six years ago in an old grocery store from the 1840s, with very thick adobe walls. It was the Frietze Grocery Store. There was a man that came from Germany, Mr. Fritz, and he intermarried with the locals, and the name evolved to Frietze, so our landlord is Roberto Frietze. He's the former mayor of Mesilla. He's very youthful in his thinking. We're in this old adobe that everyone loves, with its incredible walls—we painted them red, rosa mexicana, and ochre. It's a beautiful place. People from México and from all across the world are coming in to the bookstore. They want Sandra Cisneros's *Caramelo* in English and in Spanish. There was a man from Italy that was looking for . . . *y no se lo tragó la tierra.* We have many Germans; they're at Fort Bliss, El Paso. We have an incredible German population and nobody is meeting their needs in books. I was recently telling Lee Bird, who was at Festiba, the literary festival that I'm just coming from in Edinburgh [Texas] at Pan American University, "Lee, you haven't done any books in German." Here you are in El Paso and they have many bilingual books. They just translated a wonderful French book called *El Gran Viaje del Señor Caca.* My husband [Daniel Zolinsky] translated the *Long Journey of Mr. Poop.* It's what happens when you eat an apple, and it's a wonderful tale about the digestive system for children. It's fabulous. He also translated another book for them, *Le Petit*

Zizi. It's about a little boy who for the first time discovers his zizi. These are fabulous books for children. In fact, I just finished a children's book about two months ago. After I wrote the taco book, my father came to me in a dream and he said, "Where's my book?" and so I wrote a book called *Chano's Dream*—my father was Epifanio "Chano" Chávez. I call it an AA book. It has a double meaning—all ages, and, as you read in the book, my father was an alcoholic. It's a book that talks about the world that he grew up in, Chiva Town, where all the goats ran wild in that little barrio in Las Cruces. Even though he came from there and I come from that world, I am a global border person.

EMJ: *The small towns of your fiction, Cabritoville and Agua Oscura, are global spaces inhabited by Filipino missionaries, Iranian scholars like Mohammed, Korean shop owners, and so on. Does this diversity foster global understanding?*
DC: Oh yes, very much so. My mother was a global person, even though she didn't really go to Europe or travel that much. My parents' world was small in a certain way. But she studied in México for thirteen summers; she read vociferously, both my parents were incredible readers. My mother always had the news tuned to the world, and she was a universal person, a global person. So was my aunt, even though she grew up in this very small town, Redford, Texas, but the world was there with the books. My cousin, who later became a priest, spoke eight languages and studied in Rome. It all started with my grandmother Antonia, who was in that covered wagon, who could see across the plains; she had a vision that was very far-reaching. That was a gift; that truly was a gift.

EMJ: *One of the other things that intrigues me about your books and some of your theater plays, especially the* Novena Narrativas y Ofrendas Nuevomexicanos, *are the ways in which you transgress against the rules of genre. What is it that is so confining that you feel the need to constantly push and stretch and go against those rules?*
DC: I love to do that. I'm a rebel rouser, my dear. Even in *Face of an Angel*, the chapter that has two voices was so confounding to people, but I realized that the people that asked that question on the chapter with the voices had never read a theater piece, never read a play, because you can have two, three, four, however many voices speaking at the same time. I have a theater degree; I am an actor. That has informed me in many ways. It's made me a writer

of characterization and voice. As a theater person, I feel that it's given me the gift of action, of being able to see the stage set, moving people through space, hearing voices, also seeing movement in a very detailed way because when you're writing a play, you're the director, you're the actor, you're the set designer, and I had done all these things in theater. I worked at the Dallas Theater Center for three years. I was in the costume shop, I worked lights, I did sound, I prepared the food, I was a prop person, I did laundry, I sewed costumes, I've done everything, and that gives you an overall panoramic view of the playing field. Sometimes the voices or the scene is dictated by what needs to be done.

I was just reviewing a play I've written called *Plague-Time* that has never seen the light. It's a play about the bubonic plague. I've always been interested in the Middle Ages and the bubonic plague, and in Nuevo México we have still many instances of plague, particularly up around Santa Fe. So I did a lot of research and wrote a musical called *Plague-Time*. Writing it was a good experience. The thing that confounds me is that I actually have two plays. I wrote one version and then I wrote another version, and they're totally different plays. I think we should do one one night and the other one another night. They're the same play, but they have two different angles. It's like a gemstone, sometimes it catches the light that way and then you want to move it this way. That's how I see creativity. Some things lend themselves to theater; some things are short stories, but I like to play around. I am like Sam Shepard. He called theater "play," and in a way you're playing around and moving things around, so I purposely in *Face of an Angel* bent a lot of forms, more than in anything else except for maybe *Taco Testimony*. You're not used to seeing consejos or recetas; the recipes are all real, but I've never written a cookbook. I'm not sure if you need half a teaspoon of this or that, so I do my approximation. Then again you have a poem, and then you have a prayer. The prayers surprised me. I didn't realize there were so many prayers to be prayed—prayers before eating tacos, prayers for comida, and so on and so forth. I think that's the magic of writing. But from the very beginning of my writing career there was criticism; people were confounded by my lack of plot. I've constantly been jumped at for that, and you know what, I don't care anymore. My work has a different sense of time and place and sensibility. What is a plot? I'm not sure. Maybe I was missing that day in school. I don't know. It's just like the day I missed multiplication tables—seven eights has always confounded me, seven times eight, eight times nine—I must have been absent that day. Something happened to me when plot was discussed. Or perhaps my plots are different.

NS: *Have you had trouble getting published because of this?*
DC: I haven't so far. We'll see how it goes with my new novel, *The King and Queen of Comezón.* I've been working on that piece for over twenty years. Comezón is an itch literally, but it's also a longing that you can't satisfy. I feel that it's some of my best writing ever. The protagonist has worked in government, the border patrol. I'm glad to be here in front of [a picture of] Gloria Anzaldúa because in a way I work in the tradition of Gloria Anzaldúa. I see that most Chicana and Latina writers are writing about the obvious, and it's not an unkind statement. I mean how many more books do we need on las mujeres de Juárez? Yes we do because it's a reality. The drug cartel is going crazy. There have been a lot of murders, yes, yes, yes, but Gloria had an overview. She had that global perspective that you're talking about that I want to have as well. The border is where the strength of *Canícula* comes from—the border, the whole Laredo world of Norma Cantú. I feel I am in that same tradition, walking hand in hand with Gloria, whom I knew very well, and I loved what she did; I loved that reality she had that reached out so far. She had an incredible mind. I feel my book *Comezón* has that global view of the border, and I think there are more things to be talked about than just the women of Juárez, for whom we advocate very much in our cultural center. We sell these beautiful huipils made in Chiapas that say, "Amigos de las mujeres de Juárez." We sell T-shirts that say "Make Tacos Not War"; we have "No Border Wall" T-shirts, and I have to tell you when I wear that shirt nobody looks at me; I become invisible.

EMJ: *I think you'd find a lot of sympathy for that sentiment in South Texas.*
DC: Yes, and people don't realize not only is it going to impact human beings; it's impacted the Tohono O'Odham in Arizona, the elders that are bringing their sacred rattles over, animal life, the migratory trail, and the whole environmental impact. Now our struggles are in El Paso, Las Cruces, and Juárez. The tri-city area has formed an alliance to work on binational concerns. We're very concerned about the Santa Teresa border crossing and Lomas del Poleo.[2] There's a lot of devastation taking place right now in the neighborhood of Segundo Barrio,[3] and we have a Segundo Barrio T-shirt with a raised fist. There's a billionaire from Santa Fe that has come into

El Paso and has gentrified the neighborhood and is destroying a lot of the property. These binational entities, very wealthy people, families from Juárez and from the U.S., and our own governor in New Mexico have built up this whole new border. The new border is at Santa Teresa, and they're changing neighborhoods and moving things around, oftentimes to the detriment of the locals.

If I had stayed in academia, I probably would not have gotten so involved in community, but now I'm in the trenches of community, working with undocumented people. The aunt of one of our trade show coordinators for our festival was deported on some technicality, even though she'd lived in the U.S. for thirty years, and the only way she could protest was from jail. The only way she could get a lawsuit going was by being in jail; she preferred not to do that, so she moved back to México. You may have heard of the deportations in Chaparral and Gadsden and how the sheriff's department would go up to a home and say, "Oh we heard you called 911," only to find out the family had no phone. Once they would get inside the house, they would deport people because they were undocumented. So we're on the firing line—there is firing going on but not from us. We don't want that. The idea is getting back to the border as Gloria Anzaldúa conceived and meant the border to be; it is a place of great transformation and change and we're living it right now. It's not only our border. We think we're the only border, but what's happening in France? What's happening in Iraq? Look at all the borders in the world. So we are just part of the globalization of evil and war, and we need as global citizens to address these issues.

EMJ: *In your novels you write about the common cross-border traffic—families going to market, visiting each other, Mara in* Face of an Angel *going to find her father in Mexico, or buying things for the blue room in Mexico. Has all that changed since 2001?*
DC: It has for a lot of people, but I go over to Juárez all the time. I buy groceries and papayas and go to Sanborns to eat fideos and to buy books. Our government has created terror with the levels of alert. I don't listen to those things. I try to promote peace. Yes, one should be careful. I'm not going to be out someplace at two in the morning. But yes, some people have been terrified, and they have shut down. For many of us, the border is our playing field and our landscape and we love it. We are working to heal it, and to do that you have to participate in life just as a woman in Iraq would go out

and get bread; you have to be out there. If you're in the marketplace and the bomb goes off . . . I hate to think of all the people that have died, the civilians, the mothers, the children, but you have to go on with life.

NS: *You are currently protesting the building of a border wall. You were at the University of New Mexico when there were a number of dramatic changes taking place in the United States, during the Chicano movement when the term "Chicano" was taking on a whole new meaning. At that time, the late sixties and early seventies, were you actively involved in that movement?*
DC: I was in the theater department for a long time, and in the very early movement, I found myself lost in the world of university theater. I became more involved as time went along, but I think it was a raising of consciousness. That's what I say when people ask me what is a Chicano or a Chicana—it is someone with a political consciousness. My consciousness was always awakened by my mother, who was a great humanitarian, taking food and clothing to people in Juárez, working with the needy, and helping little viejitas. She had an old lady she took care of. We always had students from México that lived with us. We were always involved in helping human beings. I remember marching in Santa Fe when Somoza visited. As I moved through my own consciousness, which was evolving through time, I became more active. When I moved to Española [Northern New Mexico Community College], I became very active and I started aligning myself with people like Estevan Arellano and some of the people from La Academia de la Nueva Raza. I knew all those people, and I got involved with them. That was a great consciousness awakening for me, and I never really have articulated what moving to northern New Mexico did for me. I was the director of the drama department there. That was a great awakening too. Even at the Dallas Theater Center when I was a graduate student with Paul Baker, I happened to be in an ethnic theater company, and I saw a lot of injustices there. I was very unhappy with the way ethnic people were treated and myself in particular. I had to battle with that, and I was always a bit of a rebel. I was also working as a waitress at the Steak and Ale. I would work the lunch shift and then I'd go home and watch Dialing for Dollars and work on my thesis. It took me three years to get out of there, but out of my class of maybe thirty-five people that started, there were only two of us that actually got our Masters at the end of that period, and it was in great pains too because there was a lot of hypocrisy for me in that particular department.

It was a time of struggle. I had applied for a job and I had not really experienced that kind of racism. I remember that I went for a job and a woman said to me, "You know your people have such beautiful hair," which seemed like an inoffensive comment but now that I reflect on it, it has meant more to me. I actually was able to write about that later, a piece about hair, and this came back to me because I was doing a reading in New York City and I wanted to have my hair done at Elizabeth Arden or one of those places. They assigned me a Latino Puerto Rican guy, and I felt troubled by a lot of things. It was an awakening consciousness that probably has been a lifetime movement leading to where I am right now.

I find myself really being able to kick ass now because I understand the world better. If you put yourself in a position to understand deeply the sorrows of the world, it makes you stronger because then you can help people. I'm not going to say that it happened all at once. Part of it was observing my mother, observing my father and how he was treated, or listening to his stories of growing up in Chiva Town, and how they couldn't speak Spanish in the school yards. When my mother passed on, while cleaning her attic I saw a newspaper because she saved them floor to ceiling—I went through every single newspaper in her attic and there was a picture of undocumented workers being shackled and being paraded through the downtown streets of Las Cruces in the late thirties. I thought, "I can't believe this. This is my hometown. I cannot believe this." They had a camp for Japanese families as well and yet we grew up with the Nakayamas and the Tashiros. They were our local farmers and as much a part of our community as anyone else. There was a lot of injustice, but it was a gradual consciousness empowerment.

NS: *In your books you portray this sense of a cultural third space for Mexican Americans. They're not Mexican and they're not accepted as Anglos. You use the expression "deracinated."*
DC: That's not all people though; that was my father.

NS: *In* Loving Pedro Infante, *one of the criticisms that Mexican Americans have for each other is, "Oh, you sound too Mexican, you look too Mexican." Are such prejudices among Mexican Americans less tolerable to you than those that Mexican Americans endure from Anglo Americans?*
DC: I don't like racism or intolerance. Who would as a human being? When we injure one, we injure all. I was able to observe that in my own family. I

remember a family member coming up one time and my father was wearing a guayabera, and she said, "Why don't you put him in something else? He looks so Mexican." She grew up away from us in Colorado and she didn't have the culturization that we did. She came back without a lot of the depth of culture we had living with my mother. I found it very difficult to understand how anybody could criticize a cactus; she didn't like the cactus in my garden—too Mexican. What I tried to do in *A Taco Testimony* was present two aspects—my mother's family and my father's family. My mother's family got ahead. My mother's sister was Texas Mother of the Year. They have this plaque on the campus of the first Hispano graduates. My father's family has done very well. My father was a graduate of Georgetown University. Some of the family members did very well, but his brother was a janitor, and they always looked down on him. Then there was the language issue. So I was in between, in between borders of people, but I never really lost my center, my core, whoever I was, because my mother had solidified that within us very deeply. We knew where we came from, we knew who we were, we knew what our languages were, and I just thank God for my mother's integrity, her wisdom, and her backbone because I was able to see the difference between one side of the street and the other side of the street. At my cousin's birthday party, I was sitting next to another cousin who taught art for a few years in the schools, but she didn't know what a milagro was, you know the prayer amulet, and I said I can't believe this. She's an artist! We on one street knew what art and culture was, but then again on the next street over there was no understanding of Mexican art and no culture.

NS: *Your mother was an art student, wasn't she?*
DC: No, she was a language student. She studied Spanish, but she took art classes and studied with Diego Rivera. My older sister recalls Frida Kahlo. She says that she always smelled because she smoked incessantly. She remembers them very well because they were friends of Dolores del Río and that whole clique. My mother was incredibly beautiful. I look very much like her, but I've not fulfilled her criteria—wear your hair back. She always had her molote, her bun, her red lipstick, and her red nail polish, even in her seventies, and her mandate was, "Are you wearing a bra?" "Yes, I am, Mom." She was an incredible human. You see her picture on the *Taco Testimony*, a beautiful woman, strong, rigid, moralistic, but she was also great humanitarian. I learned from the best.

EMJ: *Did you have fun immersing yourself in Pedro lore?*

DC: Absolutely! I started off with a pain in my heart. I wanted to write about love, deceiving love, and the angst of loving the wrong person. I have a whole other version of the book and I showed it to my editor and he said, "Too dark." I refer to that as the espresso version. I then rewrote the book, and what you have there is the latte version. The other one was really too dark. It was first person, but it was like this gigantic head in a room. I call it the "talking head" version, and it's unlikely that anyone will see it until I pass on, but it was fun.

I just can't recall that moment in which Pedro clicked in there, but we used to spend the weekends going to see the movies with my mother. We'd go to the white theater in El Paso, and we'd see *Imitation of Life* with Lana Turner, and then we'd go down to El Colón, the Spanish-language movie house, so I was always in between those worlds of la frontera, the border. It was a very cultural experience and I loved it, but I think it was divinely ordained that Pedro would have come into this because I don't think the book would have had quite the impact that it's had. I've been able to talk to Irma Infante and work with the family. When the book first came out in México, they wanted to sue me because they thought it was about Pedro, and my editor got a call from Editorial Planeta, the Mexican publishing house, thinking I had written a book about Pedro Infante.

That tour was a highlight of my life—to tour México with the book *Loving Pedro Infante* and to be on the Zócalo at the book festival, El Festival del Libro del Zócalo! It was a dream come true. It was the most incredible book tour. It was an intense two weeks; I have never worked so hard. They put me in a room with about forty sales reps and that was probably the worst time of my life. I had to talk to these men about why *they* should sell the book and what the book meant. I came out of there exhausted, but it was a great trip because I read at the studio where Pedro used to work. I was on the Pedro Infante Radio Hour; they gave me a T-shirt. A man, a personal friend of Pedro Infante, came in with a big bag, like Santa Claus, and he dumped it out on the table and there was Pedro Infante's belt buckle and a photo album. I cannot tell you the great gifts that have come to me because of that book, the people I've met. I have a museum of Pedro Infante memorabilia. An architect in New York gave me a box of clippings of the day that Pedro Infante died; they are in impeccable condition. I have original records from the Peerless label of Pedro Infante, incredible things.

Sandra Cisneros and I did a Pedro Infante event in San Antonio, and she had an artist translate a nude photo of Pedro that was taken in a shower into a charcoal drawing that's six feet by four feet. She drove it to my house in her truck. Last year, which was the homenaje of Pedro Infante's fiftieth anniversary, we had a blowout party. This year we're doing it again, the fifty-first anniversary. We have a Tongolele look-alike, and we're doing clips from some of her movies. We're showing *A Toda Maquina* and then we're bringing out Sandra's charcoal painting, which is bigger than life size, so it could be slightly enhanced, and we put it behind a blanket. For a dollar, you can see puro Pedro.

NS: *Puro Pedro sounds like a good fund-raising event.*
DC: Yes! What can I say? Then there were people like the woman who showed up in the theater in Los Angeles when I gave a reading, looking for Pedro Infante. She had not realized that he had been dead for forty some years. I have pictures of people weeping at our homenaje last year.

NS: *In* Loving Pedro Infante, *Tere reflects on the meaning of "macho" in Spanish and English, and she says, "My culture has suffered too much from translation."*[4] *I wonder if you could expand on this some more.*
DC: I addressed a little bit in the *Taco Testimony* what macho means in English and what it means in Spanish. In México and Latin America, to be a macho is a complimentary term because you're responsible, you're an upright human being who takes care of family and kin and all of your affairs and everything, but I think in the U.S. it has derogatory connotations. People have a concept of how Latinos should be, how women should be, and I think I've addressed that in different places—the Mexican spitfire, the bombshell, the Tongolele, and mind you Tongolele was a U.S. citizen from Washington State who moved with her family to México. I think that too often cultures are misunderstood and people have a concept of what mexicano is, of what Mexican Americans are, of how they should be, how they should behave; it's a world of too many Cinco de Mayos and Diez y Seis de Septiembres and "pull out a Coors" when in fact we mexicanos have been boycotting Coors for years. But you go to a mexicano festival, there's the Coors, there's the mound of grapes. Remember the grape boycott? I have dreaded going to Chicano events sometimes because they take you to the

worst Mexican restaurants, and then you're confronted with the stereotypical images of the serape on the wall, the lazy Mexican slumped under the cactus. It's like Native American stereotypes. I'm really sorry but I'm sick of the howling coyote and Kokopelli and all of those sorts of things. We're much deeper; our roots, our heritages, our cultures are much deeper.

NS: *And much more diverse.*

DC: And diverse, yes. That's where the machismo starts from. It's a paternalistic viewpoint that is very limited about what the essence of culture and personality and selfhood really are. But men have probably suffered the most from this, women have too, but men as well. Our men have been emasculated. It's fabulous to see a book like *Vatos* by Luis Urrea that gives praise to the men. We don't celebrate our Mexicano/Latino men enough, and that is why that book is so great. He's one of our great American writers. There are great craftsmen and great writers, and he's definitely up there with Sandra Cisneros and Victor Martínez. I'd like to see his work out there more. *Parrot in the Oven* is a great coming-of-age book. It is the counterpart to *Mango Street* [by Cisneros]. Gary Soto is a great writer; he writes so clearly, so cleanly. Ben Sáenz is a great poet. I really love *Sammy and Juliana in Hollywood.* That's one of my favorite books of his because that's our town, that's our American Graffiti. He never talks about Las Cruces enough. He grew up there, but he's become more of an El Paso writer and I've given him a hard time about that. His books are often dark. Some of the other Chicano writers are dangerous; they're young and they see themselves as young bucks. Listen, I had my time and my day but . . .

NS: *You were a child of the sixties! [laughter]*

DC: I was a child of the sixties, but at the same time I think our writing has to deepen, and we need to stand up. Our life is fleeting. I saw Tato Laviera yesterday, the great Puerto Rican poet who's gone blind from diabetes and is on dialysis, and he's still out there speaking and doing his wonderful work. Life is a finite thing. I mean what are we doing here? I'm sorry if I'm making a judgment call, but I only have so much time and I want to work with so many people and so you have to take these things into consideration. So when you're an administrator of a festival, you very carefully pick who comes and what you do.

NS: *The Border Book Festival is open to the public, right?*
DC: Yes, and we have it on the plaza [in Mesilla, New Mexico]. We have even got a lucha libre ring donated. We're having Mexican wrestling, and Xavier Garza, who's from the Valley, is reading from *Lucha Libre: The Man in the Silver Mask.* We have slam poets, children's storytelling by Amy Costales who's a children's writer, the musical group La Familia Vigil, Perla Batalla, a backup singer for Leonard Cohen from Los Angeles, and we have a free concert. It's very public and very oriented towards people. I've always worked with people that are connecting and healing. That's why Quincy Troupe has come back. Quincy is living in New York. We took him to La Casa, which is a battered women's shelter. He worked with a woman in the morning, he's a big man with dreadlocks, and he was working with little mujeres chaparritas mexicanas. He was blown away by these little women. In the afternoon we took him to the juvenile detention center and he worked with the son—the mother in the morning, the son in the afternoon. He just couldn't get over that so I know that's why he's coming back. Our artists are going out to Chaparral, Santa Teresa [New Mexico], all these little towns.

Perla Batalla is giving a major concert in Vado, New Mexico. Vado was a black settler community—there's a book here that I or somebody should write. After the civil war, there was a utopian settlement of black soldiers called Blackdom in Portales, New Mexico, but they were run out of town and then settled in Vado, which is on the way to El Paso. So when Alice Walker came to the festival the second year, we were able to connect her with Mitch Boyer and his family in Blackdom. There're also many Chinese in El Paso. El Paso Street, where El Colón Theater is, saw a wave of Lebanese move in, and you still see a lot of Lebanese people in El Paso, and Chinese. As a matter of fact, there's a restaurant where they sell tortas in front of the Colón Theater, and they were digging that up and found a body of a very small person. It turned out to be a Chinese woman. El Colón was built on the burial site of a Chinese cemetery. Now you see the Koreans. To me, this mestizaje is wonderful.

EMJ: *Why do you tend to juxtapose New Mexico and West Texas? What are the dynamics there?*
DC: There was never any boundary. You take a little chalupa, the little canoe, and you go across if you need to take wood from here to there to build

a little house. I never felt any boundaries; I never felt I was connected to the United States. It was a great relief to be in an environment that was so free and so open and so vast and to see yourself against that landscape. That was my mother's world when she was growing up. Her great-grandfather had gotten that land grant to move over, and so they were citizens of both worlds. That is my world. Mesilla, New Mexico, two miles from Las Cruces, was México before the Gadsden Purchase. So you are right smack dab in the middle of México, but now it's defined by Nuevo México and Texas. The worlds were very different—New Mexico growing up with my father, coming to Texas to be with my mother's people, and then going from a defined space to an undefined space. There is a thesis here for somebody just to talk about spatial realities. I need to write an essay about the difference between northern and southern New Mexico. Their patron saint is La Conquistadora and ours is Our Lady of Guadalupe. I lived in Santa Fe for seven years and I loved it; I did very well and it's a wonderful place. My sister lives there, but it's not la frontera. I am a border woman and so I'm talking about going through different worlds and different universes and different realities. Texas is a totally different space. Balmorhea, Fort Davis, Marfa, Presidio where my aunt lived, those are sacred places. There's a documentary of that part of the world called *The Devil's Swing*, and it has an actual limpia, a spirit cleansing, and some narcocorridos in it. Have you read *The Devil in Texas?* It was written in the sixties by Aristeo Brito, a cousin of mine. It's about Presidio, Texas, and it is a study of generations of people in the small town of Presidio. The book is in the tradition of *Pocho* and is now a classic in Chicano literature. It's a major indictment of racism, but it follows the generations. Aristeo lives in Tucson and teaches at Pima Community College; he plays the guitar, he's an incredible performer, and he sings. About three years ago, we gave him our Premio Fronterizo, our highest award for people who have transcended borders, real and imagined. He's an incredible reader/performer but he's one example of a man who has never gotten enough glory.

SELECTED WORKS BY DENISE CHÁVEZ

Books

A Taco Testimony: Meditations on Family, Food and Culture. Tucson: Rio Nuevo Publishers, 2006.

La Ultima Muchacha del Menú. New York: Vintage Español, 2005.

The Last of the Menu Girls. Houston: Arte Público Press, 1984. Republished, New York: Vintage, 2004.

Loving Pedro Infante. New York: Farrar, Straus and Giroux, 2001. Republished, New York: Washington Square Press, 2001.

Face of an Angel. New York: Farrar, Straus and Giroux, 1994.

Children's Book
La Mujer Que Sabía El Idioma de Los Animales/The Woman Who Knew the Language of the Animals. New York: Houghton Mifflin Press, 1993.

Plays
"Novena Narrativas y Ofrendas Nuevo Mexicanas." In *Chicana Creativity and Criticism: New Frontiers in American Literature,* edited by María Herrera-Sobek and Helena María Viramontes, 85–100. Houston: Arte Público Press, 1988.

Plague-Time, 1984.

Women in the State of Grace (one-woman show), 1989.

NOTES

1. Denise Chávez, *Face of an Angel* (New York: Warner Books, 1994), 4.
2. Lomas del Poleo is a disputed area outside of Juárez. Local families are trying to block developers from taking over, but they are being harassed by private guards hired by a wealthy developer. Lomas del Poleo gained international attention in 1996 when it was the dumping ground for the bodies of raped and murdered women. For more information see http://pasodelsur.com.
3. Segundo Barrio, in El Paso, is a site of land disputes with border developers. For more information, see http://pasodelsur.com.
4. Denise Chávez, *Loving Pedro Infante* (New York: Washington Square Press, 2001), 52.

INDEX